ULTIMATE PERFORMANCE

Measuring Human Resources at Work

NICHOLAS C. BURKHOLDER
with SCOTT GOLAS and JEREMY SHAPIRO

BICENTENNIAL
1807
WILEY
2007
BICENTENNIAL

John Wiley & Sons, Inc.

Library of Congress Cataloging-in-Publication Data:
Burkholder, Nicholas C.
    Ultimate performance : measuring human resources at work / Nicholas C.
Burkholder.
      p. cm.
    ISBN 978-0-471-74121-3 (cloth)
    1. Performance—Measurement. 2. Organizational effectiveness—
Measurement. 3. Employees—Rating of. 4. Performance standards. 5.
Strategic planning—Evaluation. I. Title.
HF5549.5.P37B87 2007
658.3'125—dc22
                                                          2006032783

Printed in the United States of America.

10 9 8 7 6 5 4 3 2

To the trailblazers:

Jac Fitz-enz
Robert Kaplan
David Norton
David Ulrich
Mark Huselid
Brian Becker

And Gary Cluff, John Sullivan, Gerry Crispin,
Tony Lee, Lynn Nemser, and the other early
contributors to staffing metrics.

Contents

Preface

S omewhere in nearly every organization's annual report, C-level executives remark that employees are "the most important asset" in the organization. Until recently, that's where notice of this incredibly valuable asset stopped. The executives believed that accurate measurement of the management of this asset was impossible. Now most know it is possible, but find that their organizations are not adequately equipped to measure the performance of the department with the greatest responsibility for that asset: Human Resources. Making informed decisions regarding critical Human Capital-related issues like the acquisition, development, and deployment of employees is of paramount importance to the ongoing success of any organization.

Many areas of executive decision making are indeed supported by sophisticated, time-tested tools and methodologies. Finance and marketing are now considered to be hard core sciences. The systems in place make use of a wide variety of metrics gathered internally and externally on inputs, processes, and outputs relevant to the business of the organization. The framework underlying these systems is relevant to almost every part of the organization. So why then is the one asset base of any organization without which it cannot exist—its employees—allowed to escape this measured scrutiny?

What is needed is an approach that integrates the measurement of Human Capital assets (and not just the cost of their acquisition) into the decision support models used by finance and operational executives. The Finance department is responsible for providing the tools and methodology related to implementing strategies that support the mission and objectives of the organization. So too, the Human Resources department should be responsible for the development of tools and methodologies relevant to Human Capital assets and their place in the organizational mission, objectives, and strategy. This represents a significant new level of responsibility for the Human Resources department and those who work within it. Along with this additional responsibility will come greater accountability and an opportunity to elevate the perception of Human Resources to the science it is.

To make matters easier, many of the measurement tools needed by Human Resources already exist and simply await implementation. We know that C-level executives want to know more about what Human Resources is doing to support the overall performance of the organization; metrics, the right metrics, can quickly and easily show them that their statement to shareholders about the value of their employee assets is completely accurate.

This book outlines the ways, means, and actual metrics that can transform the perception of Human Resources in any organization. Not just a cost center, Human Resources is a critical player in the improvement of organizational performance when it comes to the management of Human Capital. When metrics are used as a means of measuring and improving the performance of Human Resources in the mission, objectives, and strategy of an organization, it becomes a clear contributor to the bottom line. Case studies from top organizations complement the provided framework with solid examples of what works, what doesn't work, and how to learn from the process. If followed, the counsel of this book will give you the necessary tools to improve work, people, and performance in your organization.

Introduction

As if they didn't already face incredible challenges, 300 years ago ships were unable to accurately measure their east–west position. Getting lost was common and many ships disappeared, ran aground, or sank because they could not measure longitude. The costs in life, property, and performance were immense until 1760, when a contest underwritten by the British crown drove the development of a solution.

Human resource performance is the measurement challenge of our time and the implications are analogous to that of longitude. While organizations will quickly benefit from measuring HR correctly, it's important to understand what we've been doing wrong and why HR measurement has lagged well behind that of other organization functions.

Senior executives used to consider HR as a "soft" unavoidable cost of doing business that handled executive compensation, processed employment transactions, hosted employee functions, dealt with employee problems, and, they hoped, minimized lawsuits. Three factors changed this perception: the significant impact of high performance HR, the implications of poor performing HR, and soaring HR operating expenses. This top down demand for HR metrics has faced a number of inextricably linked challenges:

- The metrics that we've been using are fundamentally flawed, and because they're flawed they don't make a positive difference, and because they don't make a positive difference all HR measurement is undermined. These metrics include the ubiquitous yet meaningless ratio of HR to total employees and the common, yet invalid, cost-per-hire.

- Although some consultants have made substantial contributions to HR metrics, the proprietary nature of consulting is in dissonance with developing meaningful metrics. HR metrics should not be exclusive to clients, and many consultants espouse too many metrics and metrics that are too complex to be of practical value. Some consultants also exploit organizations' obsession with strategy and focus on measuring strategy, while organizations should be focusing on measuring objectives and outcomes.

- The HR profession was slow to initiate measurement, and the first initiatives were process and not outcome oriented.

Before we set out to measure HR at work we must understand what metrics are and are not. Metrics are not an end in themselves, but in the end they must be calculated. Metrics are the ultimate arbitrator and should be the final judge of performance. It is important to recognize however, that not all numbers are metrics. Real metrics:

- Measure results associated with customer defined performance objectives.

- Are limited to three to five specific metrics for any outcome or result.

- Drive continuous performance improvement.

- Are easy to calculate.
- Are easy to compare.
- Are periodically reviewed and refined.

This is not the first substantial work on HR metrics. All of us are greatly indebted to the continuing leadership of Jac Fitz-enz, the undisputed father of HR metrics. David Ulrich has always encouraged HR measurement and incorporated metrics into his unparalleled work. Additionally, Robert Kaplan, David Norton, Brain Becker, and certainly Mark Huselid are contributing greatly to this work.

Let's get to the task at hand, if for no other reason than measuring, just measuring, improves performance.

Imperatives of Metrics

Metrics of Business

As the new economic paradigm continues to recognize people as a company's key competitive advantage, Human Resources managers are required to deliver services that are not only efficient and effective but also support their organization's strategy and objectives. It's no longer sufficient for the Human Resources function just to drive down costs; rather it must also help the organization create value and differentiate itself from competitors. In today's economy, it's the human capital in organizations that will be the differentiator and ultimately decide how an organization performs. To that end, Human Resource managers play an instrumental role in helping their organizations perform by providing HR deliverables that address the human capital issues that are key to executing the business strategy. This includes utilizing metrics to gauge the performance of deliverables and the impact they have on supporting the organization in executing its strategy. It has been well documented that in this new role, Human Resources should be positioned and designed as a strategic business partner that participates in both strategy formulation and implementation. And this requires Human Resources to be aligned with the business strategy so that the appropriate deliverables and metrics are implemented. The prerequisites for an organization's human capital to be effectively aligned with its business strategy are further discussed in Chapter 2, A Path to Alignment, which identifies three fundamental steps.

DEFINE AND UNDERSTAND THE BUSINESS STRATEGY

The first factor cited is a shared and well developed understanding of an organization's strategy among business and human resource managers. It is still commonplace to find organizations that have not yet articulated and/or shared a clear mission and objectives with their workforce. In fact, a study by Mankins & Steele (2005), which surveyed senior executives in more than 197 companies worldwide, found a poorly communicated strategy as the second highest reason cited by executives as the reason for why their companies underperform. And part of the poor communication is because in many organizations the discussion still focuses on what the strategy and objectives consist of rather than how to implement them, ending up with vague and generic business objectives. Human Resource leaders can serve an important role here and establish it as a key strategic partner by facilitating how the business strategy and subsequent objectives will be implemented in their organizations.

IDENTIFY HUMAN CAPITAL DELIVERABLES THAT IMPACT THE BUSINESS

Once the business strategy and subsequent objectives are well understood, the organization can establish how its human capital will help implement the strategy and impact its objectives. The importance of such a linkage was greatly popularized by Larry Bossidy and Ram Charan's landmark book *Execution: The Discipline of Getting Things Done*, which based an organization's success on its ability to execute its business objectives. Bossidy and Charan argue that three core processes—people, strategy, and operations—and the degree to which they are linked are at the heart of providing an organization the competitive discipline needed to execute and succeed in today's marketplace. (See Figure 1.1.)

Bossidy and Charan emphasize that the people process is more important than either the strategy or operation processes, arguing that if the people process is not done right the organization will never fulfill its potential. Based on their vast experience and research with successful companies, Bossidy and Charan emphasize that getting the people process right involves integrating and linking it with business strategy and operations. They base this on a set of building blocks that leaders must use to effectively design, install, and operate the people process, as follows:

- Linkage to the strategic plan and its near (0–2 years), medium (2–5 years), and long-term (5+ years) milestones and the operating plan target, including specific financial targets.
- Developing the leadership pipeline through continuous improvement, succession depth, and reducing retention risk.
- Deciding what to do about nonperformers.
- Transforming the mission and operations of HR.

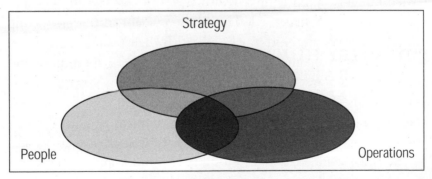

Figure 1.1

In essence, it's the first building block that links people to the strategy and operations. Bossidy and Charan argue that business leaders create this linkage by making sure they have the right kinds and numbers of people to execute the strategy. And meeting the medium and long-term milestones depends on having a pipeline of promising and promotable leaders. Only after reviewing your human capital in regard to an ability to execute the strategy will you be able to identify the specific human capital needs that must be addressed to allow the organization to achieve its objectives. But it doesn't stop there. Human Resource professionals have an opportunity to identify specific human capital deliverables that can support the accomplishment of business objectives. For example, let's say a given company has an objective to introduce a new product line as part of its business strategy, and its subsequent review of its human capital indicates that the current talent pool and its internal pipeline are sufficient to meet this objective. But let's say that, as HR professionals of this given company, we also know that our staff with product expertise is highly sought after, both from within the company and by external competitors. Any turnover would seriously impede the achievement of this objective. Seeing such a connection would prompt us to design incentives like bonuses or other reward programs that would encourage and retain staff until the objective is achieved.

These kinds of human capital deliverables can be identified when human capital is linked with how the business strategy and objectives are implemented. This is also evident in the pioneering work of Kaplan and Norton who, through their balanced scorecard approach, help organizations implement their business strategy and provide a way to measure the organization's progress toward achieving its goals. The premise of their approach is to measure business performance based on how the strategy is implemented (utilizing a strategy "map") rather than solely on what the strategy consists of.

As in the work cited by Bossidy and Charan, Kaplan and Norton found successful organizations to have a clearly defined business strategy and human capital to be integrated with the implementation process of their strategy. The balanced scorecard is essentially a framework that provides a more balanced view of organizational performance by providing other measures than the traditional financial ones, including measures regarding internal processes, customers, and an organization's human capital. It recognizes that people are related to improving business processes that deliver more value to customers, ultimately leading to increased revenue. By utilizing multiple measures, both financial and nonfinancial, the scorecard ensures that managers don't just rely on the limiting view of financial statements, which are inherently backward-looking, in assessing the performance of the organization. It is this balanced scorecard framework that pioneered moving beyond mere monitoring of financials, and actively engaged employees with the strategy implementation process of their organization. By specifying the vital measures, assessing them, and regularly communicating the organization's performance on these criteria to employees, managers ensure that the entire organization participates in strategy implementation. Although the balanced scorecard framework identified human capital as a key performance driver in the implementation of strategy, it did not specify how to measure the specific impact these deliverables will have on organizational performance. This leads us to the next and final part for alignment—assessing the contribution of human capital deliverables in implementing the business strategy and ultimately to an organization's bottom line.

MEASURE THE IMPACT OF HR DELIVERABLES

The emergence of the HR Scorecard concept, preempted by the now classic work of Becker, Huselid, and Ulrich in *The HR Scorecard: Linking People, Strategy & Performance* (2001), greatly advanced the ability to measure how human capital deliverables contribute to an organization's success. HR functions continue to struggle with appropriate and meaningful measures to quantify their value, and the HR scorecard provides a measurement tool that distinguishes among the many HR deliverables and their influence in implementing the business strategy. The HR scorecard typically complements an organization's balanced scorecard, and many of the HR scorecards in practice utilize the standard four measurement dimensions—financial, process (operations), customer, and people/human capital management (strategy)—in their HR scorecard design. In the past, HR has focused primarily on operations and as such the most often utilized metrics have involved measuring processes in terms of cost, quality, and cycle time. Clearly, HR must excel at these but when HR is viewed as a strategic partner, these types of measures provide little insight into the value HR adds nor its linkage to a company's business strategy. The HR scorecard provides the HR function with a model to measure the performance of people practices from multiple perspectives. The real challenge is for HR to produce a scorecard that contains metrics that generate value-related information so that it can measure the impact of its deliverables on the business.

Outsourcing: A Perfect Example

Metrics are an important factor in all aspects of an organization. A perfect example of how metrics apply to Human Resources is in outsourcing. By closely examining the metrics of outsourcing and applying these principles throughout other functions, the importance of metrics can be fully realized.

While modern outsourcing has been developing for some 50 years, there are still problems associated with many outsourced operations. Despite the best of intentions and planning, there will be times when things will go wrong.

It's not always right to outsource; outsourcing doesn't always work. Sometimes outsourcing may have been the right decision, but the process and/or execution were flawed. We have identified five imperatives that address the problems associated with out-sourcing. Acting on them will optimize your outsourcing perfor-mance and eliminate the failures.

1. Organization leaders should focus on objectives, not strategy.
2. More and better performance metrics must be developed.
3. Organizations should approach all "resourcing" decisions holistically.
4. Human Resources should assume responsibility for all human capital aspects of outsourcing.
5. Resourcing decisions should be based on performance.

Organization Leaders Should Focus on Objectives, Not Strategy

Our obsession with strategy is sorely misguided. Many executives make the mistake of thinking "If our strategy is clearly determined, nothing can go wrong." That line of thinking has sunk many an outsourcing ship.

So many books, speeches, presentations, and consultants are fo-cused on strategy. It's no wonder that the business world has be-come obsessed with that word. In the foreword to a popular business book, the authors note that they always "start with the same simple question, 'What is your strategy?'"

That should never be the first question. Putting strategy first will produce the same results as ready, fire, aim. The right order is:

1. Mission.
2. Objectives.
3. Strategy.

Strategy has always been third; never first. And the more emphasis that is put on mission and objectives, the easier it will be to develop the strategy.

"If you get the objectives right, a lieutenant can write the strategy" is most often credited to General George Marshall. He was an extraordinary military leader and the recognized architect of the Allied victory in World War II. But Marshall also believed in the importance of objectives when he was Secretary of State and architect of the rebuilding of Europe, President of the Red Cross, and Secretary of Defense. A recipient of the Nobel Peace Prize, George Marshall was undisputedly one of the most effective leaders of the twentieth century.

Although military leaders are responsible for this approach, it isn't just a military thing. We have worked with private and public organizations around the world. They include the elite and the mundane, the large and the small. Invariably, ineffective organizations do not have clear objectives. During an effectiveness engagement in Atlanta the CEO of a national professional services firm became ever more exasperated as he heard his nine direct reports articulate nine noticeably different mission statements and struggle with their own department's objectives. Leaders of the core functions in highly profitable organizations are invariably obsessed with their objectives, but they have met with vice presidents of functions supporting them of that may talk strategy but are not able to articulate their department's objectives. The surest way to improve any organization's performance is to take the time to get the objectives right. Employees at any level that do not know and understand the purpose of the organization and its objectives will not perform effectively, and they certainly will not be able to make the best decisions about outsourcing—or anything else.

Many of us, however, are responsible for executing, and the strategy is rightfully left to us. No significant activity should be initiated without a strategy, but it is impossible to determine an effective one unless it is derived from clear, specific objectives. Here is a simple way to get to the strategy:

1. Verify or define the mission—the main purpose for which an organization exists. The mission should make sense to management, employees, and customers. Missions are relatively long term oriented. For most businesses they should also be valid tomorrow, next month, and for at least a year. If there is some doubt about the mission, then take time to make sure everyone is on the same page.

2. Establish objectives—the specific and measurable deliverables that are essential to fulfilling the mission. Objectives should be customer driven if not jointly established and also clear to management, employees, and customers. Most importantly, objectives must be measurable.

3. Now the optimum strategy—the systematic plan of action to attain specific objectives—can be developed.

Those who have the responsibility for executing must also have the authority to adjust or even change the strategy in response to what they experience as they work towards achieving their objectives. We should also note that a strategy is no more than words unless the execution of the strategy includes the requisite structure, resources, processes, and procedures or tactics.

Establishing the right objectives is the first responsibility of leaders. Leave the strategy to those responsible for executing.

More and Better Performance Metrics Must Be Developed

Sabermetrics. It's a great word. No doubt a consulting firm would be using the term had not baseball already laid claim to it. Sabermetrics is the search for objective knowledge about baseball using mathematical and statistical analysis. Yes, after a century and a half, new metrics have been developed for this, the most measured of our pastimes.

Performance metrics are also about the search for objective knowledge using mathematical and statistical analyses. Baseball metrics help team management to make the best decisions about players and ultimately optimize the team's performance. While most organizations are more complex than a baseball team, a primary purpose of performance metrics is the same: to make the best resourcing decisions in order to optimize organizational performance.

There are no baseball metrics for strategy, player management practices, or player engagement. Even before sabermetrics, baseball statistics have always measured performance outcomes or results, as should any organization's performance statistics. Performance metrics should be associated with measurable objectives. You can't—and shouldn't try to—measure strategy or practices or engagement.

You'd think that the baseball stats that we've been using for generations have to be the best, but the data supporting sabermetrics is incredibly compelling. Michael Lewis's *Moneyball: The Art of Winning an Unfair Game* is a must read book for anyone involved in business or any aspect of human capital management. It's a compelling story about using these new metrics to build a championship-caliber team in the face of 100 years of accepted scouting practices. In spite of the data, sabermetrics have been slow to gain wide spread acceptance. *The Wall Street Journal*'s Carl Bialik reported that ". . . self interest compels veteran writers and broadcasters to reject the idea that stat heads have a better handle on the game than they do."

In business, it's the consultants and pundits who are struggling to hold on to the most overrated and useless of conventional stats. In spite of saber-sharp data, many insist there must be meaning in the metrics because they have been around for so long. The ratio of

Human Resources employees to all employees is a good example. Probably the oldest HR metric, it is based on the premise that comparing the number of HR employees to the number of total employees that they support was an indication of HR efficiency, if not performance. A ratio of 1:100 was considered the standard. Like many common metrics, it may sound logical but was flawed from inception. What if two HR organizations had the same 1:100 ratio but:

- One paid its HR staff twice as much as the other?
- One had a budget that was more than twice as big as the other?
- One supported demanding physicians and research scientists at a dozen locations around the country, while the other supported office works in one location?
- One was detested by the rest of the organization and the other was highly valued?

These are the problems with any headcount-based metrics. And yet this ratio is how many organizations manage their HR function—and HR outsourcing organizations sell their services.

The nature of functions like manufacturing and distribution fostered the development of meaningful metrics, but that is not the case for HR and human capital intensive operations indicators and performance. This perspective from major consultancy Watson Wyatt Worldwide indicates how convoluted approaches to measuring human capital indicators and performance have become:

> . . . many organizations have difficulty focusing on the "right" measures. They might measure a factor generally related to financial performance, but it may not be the best one considering the business and strategy. For example, organizations know that employee turnover is related to financial performance; and since turnover

data is readily available, a company might choose to measure turnover. But if the company's turnover rate is very low, it most likely does not strongly affect the business performance.

This suggests that a metric is important only if the data it measures is poor. If a metric is valid, it is always valid regardless of what the answer is. If turnover was a valid metric and the turnover was very low, it still should be measured. If a team measures batting averages and runs batted in, they do it regardless of whether or not the results are good or bad.

Incidentally, there are many documented cases of organizations with very low turnover that significantly and adversely affected business performance. Low turnover can be a bad thing. Retaining the wrong employees, fostering complacency, or enabling a culture that drives out change agents and high performers may result in low turnover but is deleterious to any organization. Regardless, metrics associated with turnover and cost-per-hire are as meaningless a human capital metric as the win-loss record is for pitchers. Retention—retaining the staff you want to keep—and recruiting efficiency are far better HR metrics for organizations to monitor.

Although it is often difficult to evaluate the impact of outsourcing operations because of the lack of a "before" benchmark, outsourced operations tend to be measured more than those that are not. This is because after an organization outsources work, they are more apt to ask, "What is it costing us now and what do we get for our money?" We have documented both efficient and incredibly inefficient outsourced operations. The only consistent difference between the two is that the best performers aggressively measure and report their own performance.

There is need for more and better performance metrics in every category of outsourcing but it is particularly great for human capital intensive operations. Under the auspices of Staffing.org, leading outsourcers, consultancies, academics, professional associations, and end-user organizations are working together to establish standard metrics and metrics templates to improve the measurement of human capital intensive performance. The Metrics Roundtable includes Veritude, Hewitt Associates, Saratoga, PricewaterhouseCoopers, and Watson Wyatt. These organizations are taking a leadership role in developing critical approaches and metrics for all organizations.

Until more and better performance metrics are established, keep in mind that valid metrics should:

- Be limited to no more than two to four for each outcome or result.
- Make sense to everyone associated with them.
- Be easy to understand and to measure.
- Drive continuous performance improvement.
- Be based on requirements established before initiating work.

They shouldn't be:

- Strategic—you can't measure strategy.
- Complex.
- Numerous.
- Exclusive.

A Path to Alignment

Human Resources, as a function, got its start in the personnel departments of corporate organizations in the 1930s and 1940s. The critical functions performed by the personnel department were highly process oriented and involved, for the most part, management of employee paperwork. This responsibility included oversight of a range of processes that span the entire lifecycle of an individual's employment with the company, such as the creation of job requisitions, recruitment of new hires, tracking of job applicants, orientation of new hires, management of the benefits program, performance tracking, tracking of compensation, dealing with grievances, and employee exit processing. This is just a partial list of the processes historically managed through the personnel department. The emphasis was generally on the creation and management of documentation. Every step along the path from hiring to termination needed to be carefully documented, and this huge mountain of documentation needed to be organized, filed, and tracked. In the age before modern information technology, this cataloging and tracking by itself was a daunting task. As corporations grew more complex, jobs more complicated and specialized, the personnel department continued to fill many roles and those working within the function often wore many hats.

Other functional groups such as Finance and Accounting became more and more focused within their specialty, while at the same time the personnel department, having adopted the moniker of Human Resources, took on ever more diverse tasks. A telling example is the role of the Information Technology (IT) department. One of the most significant shifts in technology measured by its impact and ubiquity has been the introduction of computers to the business organization. One of the most important early uses for computers was in the Accounting and Finance functions, and because of this, most companies put their fledgling IT departments under Finance and Accounting. Over time these departments took on ownership of other functions and assets with the organization such as communications systems and so forth. Back in the 1980s it became obvious to most that the IT group should be independent of Accounting and Finance and that managing this function from within Finance and Accounting was preventing those groups from focusing on their prime tasks. Meanwhile, the Human Resources function took on more and more responsibility in a range of areas related to employees. As a result of this, Human Resources today covers a huge range of functions from those related to talent management such as recruiting, staffing, training, leadership development, and retention as well as managing benefits, employee engagement, wellness benefits, employee legal issue management, and many others. Human Resources professionals are expected to wear a range of hats including, but not limited to:

- Performance consultant.
- Employment law expert.
- Compensation consultant.
- Change consultant.

- Designer/developer of Performance Management Systems (PMS).
- Leadership developer within an organization.
- Staffing expert.
- Human Resources reengineer.
- Trainer.
- Human Resources Information Systems administrator.

In the past, the role of the Human Resources department and the professionals within it has been limited to fulfillment and implementation. Those working within these groups were seen as "personnel specialists." That role is slowly evolving to one of human capital advisor, working as a strategic partner with senior executives on a wide variety of human capital related issues with the goal of creating and maintaining an environment for the optimal use of human capital. However, as of today, few CEOs would say that their Human Resources departments were truly strategic. Given the somewhat schizophrenic set of functions that the department is tasked with, this conclusion is not surprising.

Dr. John W. Boudreau, a professor at USC's Marshall School of Business and Research Director at the Center for Effective Organizations, and Peter M. Ramstad, Executive Vice President for Strategy and Finance at Personal Decisions International, have investigated the alignment or perceived lack thereof between Human Resources and the core business of the firm (Boudreau & Ramstad, 2001). In their research they found the frustration of executive level managers reflected in questions such as these:

- Why is there so little logical connection between our core business management processes and talent? We have well-developed strategic planning, marketing, operations, and budgeting processes that connect deeply and logically with our understanding of how to create competitive success and shareholder value. Yet, at best these core processes reflect only general talent goals like headcount, labor costs, or generic Human Resources programs. At worst, people issues don't even appear except as a headcount budget at the end of the plan.

- We invest heavily in the latest Human Resources measurement techniques—Human Resources scorecards, Human Resources financial reports, return on investment of Human Resources programs, and studies in how Human Resources programs enhance attitudes, skills, and abilities. Yet, these Human Resources measurements seldom drive key business decisions such as acquisitions and entry into new markets. Moreover, our investors can't rely on these measures to show them the competitive value of our talent. Can talent measures truly drive business decisions and investments?

When Boudreau and Ramstad discussed these issues with the Human Resources professionals at these firms they heard a matching set of frustrations, as reflected in the following questions and statements:

- The strategic mandates for the organization are clear, and we use the best processes we know to connect to them. Yet, our Human Resources strategy discussions typically focus on: (1) What Human Resources programs will we offer; (2) Should Human Resources be centralized or decentralized; (3) What IT and other infrastructure is needed to make it all work; and (4) Why it is so hard to justify the investment? (5) What is missing in our connection to the big-picture issues?
- Human Resources professionals are personally well-respected, yet as a whole our Human Resources profession lacks the respect, credibility, and impact of other core professions like Finance, Marketing, and Operations. Why is respect for Human

Resources as a whole less than the respect for Human Resources individual contributors?

- We always have a few Human Resources professionals that are trusted business contributors, respected and effective in their perspective on how talent connects to strategic success. Yet, Finance, Marketing, and Engineering routinely produce this kind of leader. In Human Resources, they are a precious few, and each has their own unique approach. Why can't we more reliably create this kind of leadership excellence across our entire group of Human Resources professionals?

Studying these perspectives, it is apparent that there is a significant mismatch between where Human Resources is today and where senior executives expect it to be. One significant item that comes up again and again is that of justification. Human Resources spends a significant portion of its time in justifying why the company should be making the investments in Human Resources related programs that are being touted. Constantly being in the position of justifying their very existence, Human Resources executives find themselves in a defensive posture. While most firms find their Finance function strategic and never consider outsourcing it, many firms are looking at the idea of significantly, or even completely, outsourcing the Human Resource function. In a recent survey by the Human Resources Metrics Consortium, the inability to document Human Resources and Human Capital performance was the primary reason for terminating Human Resources professionals.

Given the microscope that the Human Resources department often finds itself under from a cost perspective, it is instructive to keep in mind that, for most organizations, the entire cost of Human Resources that is not related to employee benefits is typically around 2 percent of revenues. This is a very small chunk of the bottom line. Reducing costs in the Human Resources department by

10 percent (a significant change in costs) would bring this to 1.8 percent; a small change in the bottom line. The point here is that there is not a great deal of leverage to be had in looking at cost reduction in the Human Resources department. A far better approach would involve looking at how Human Resources as a function can have a greater impact on the organization. For example, the ability to track and understand the issues related to employee retention in a large, low technology services firm can have a huge effect on the bottom line.

How can we determine if an organization's Human Resources department is aligned with the strategic goals and mission of the organization? This seems like a fairly straightforward question, one that must have undoubtedly been answered or at least asked repeatedly. As it turns out, this is an area of significant frustration! As a function within an organization, getting to the core involves: (1) a statement of what we are, (2) a definition of alignment, and (3) a system for determining the current level of alignment. Unfortunately, this is an area where concrete measures and models are not readily available, yet many organizations seem to be very successful at determining if particular functions within the organization are well aligned with the company's overall strategy or not. When questioned on measuring strategic alignment, many top executives will state that they can see when something is aligned and when it is not. In a very simplified view of strategic development, there are two stages: planning and implementation. No strategy is complete without these two elements.

So if the Finance department spends most of its efforts on tasks that are generally considered well aligned with the organization's strategic mission and Human Resources does not (at least in the opinion of most C-level executives in Fortune 100 companies), how can Human Resources look more like Finance, at least from the perspective of demonstrating strategic alignment? Let's start by examining how the Finance department demonstrates alignment.

Even before we get started on that, there needs to be an agreement on what strategic alignment means.

Demonstrating Alignment

Of interest in this context is the ability to demonstrate alignment with key corporate strategic objectives; such a demonstration of alignment requires three fundamental factors:

1. An understanding of the corporate strategic goals themselves. These will be unique to each organization. If well conceived and articulated, corporate goals are the shorthand description of the path to success for the firm.

2. A set of hypotheses that describe how Human Capital relates and how it can impact corporate goals. This requires a firm understanding of the role of Human Capital and the ability to develop plausible causal effect models that trace the route of the potential impacts through a chain of effects. For example, consider a cell phone service provider with a corporate goal of creating ultimate differentiation through the best customer service in the industry. There are many ways that employees play into positive customer service, one of which is training. A potential hypothesis is that better and more extensive training of customer service representatives will positively impact customer service ratings. Additional training will have a cost associated with it but should yield superior customer service. Matching these up in as quantitative an approach as possible is the heart of the modeling approach that will be discussed.

3. A clear, predefined plan for showing, in as concrete terms as possible (and appropriate), what the impacts and changes have been. This book will provide you with the tools and methodologies to tackle the second and third items above.

Human Resources Accounting: Well Intentioned, but Not Well Received

The state-of-the-art in Human Resource Accounting is Dr. Eric Flamholtz's Stochastic Rewards Valuation Model. The model develops concepts such as expected realizable value of an employee and an organization service state matrix—concepts that are best reviewed during a semester in graduate school, not in this book.

However, we can grasp the essence of the Stochastic Rewards Valuation Model. It looks at the return an employee generates through that person's entire career (for example, from retail shop assistant to assistant manager to store manager), taking into account the probability of promotion and the probability of turnover. For example, shop assistants will, on average, generate a certain return to the company. The chances that they will be promoted to a more valuable position (or quit) can also be estimated. So with a little math the value an average employee will return over, say, a ten-year period can be estimated. This is the best the field of Human Resource Accounting provides, but it is hard to imagine a firm using this except in unusual situations. It requires too much data that is not readily available. Human Resource Accounting has not made the transition from academia to practice because, to date, it has not produced methods of everyday usefulness to firms.

Supporting Human Capital Decision Making

If you are reading this book, then you are likely aware that the use of metrics in human capital management has been receiving a good deal of attention recently in a variety of forums. Many in Human Resources are ready to jump on the metrics bandwagon and are looking for specific directions on how to begin. Getting started with any new initiative can be a daunting task. The development of a metrics approach is seen as finding the best human capital related metrics (the what to measure) and deciding which measurement and analysis techniques to use (the how), as well as the methodology for interpretation (what does it mean), followed by making recommendations for appropriate action (what to do about it). With such a broad cut, the goal of developing an all encompassing metrics plan is the kind of project that can easily be measured in person years.

We have left out the most important dimension in terms of defining a metrics strategy: the why. Metrics should not be gathered, analyzed, and reported on for the sake of doing so. There needs to be an underlying motivation. Looking across the various disciplines that define most of the functional areas in modern business organizations, the underlying motivation for gathering data, analyzing, reporting on trends, and making recommendations, relates to decision support. Frequently the individuals or department responsible for providing decision support are not the same individuals making the actual decisions.

Boudreau and Ramstad have drawn a powerful analogy between where Human Resources is today in terms of human capital analytics and where Finance was 50 years ago in terms of analyzing accounting related data. In an oversimplification, accounting can be described as the function charged with the recording and reporting of all the financially related transactions that occur between an organization, its partners, customers, employees, and so on. These numbers can then be aggregated and reported on in literally millions of different ways. As expressed in the Generally Accepted Accounting Principles (GAAP) set by the Financial Accounting Standards Board (FASB), these accounting principles can be thought of as the rules governing how this is done. FASB (or any other agency) dictates exactly how the accounting numbers should be interpreted in any given situation and how that interpretation should drive financially related business decisions. This is a critical point of comparison. Accounting can produce a myriad of metrics, but without some guiding framework, or as Boudreau and his colleagues have succinctly put it, "a decision science," drawing any reasonable conclusions from this sea of numbers is nearly impossible. In the maturing discipline of Accounting and Scientific Financial Management, it does not make sense to ask, "What makes a good accounting number?" If it was asked, the answer would be in the form of another question, "What decision are you trying to support?" Modern finance as a decision science has evolved considerably in just the last five or so decades and grew out of the need to make sense of the numbers that were being generated from the accounting process.

It is important to understand the distinction between the roles of making decisions and supporting those who make the decisions. In the end, the quality of any decision support system, and the underlying metrics and analytics that it encompasses, is best measured by the quality of the supported decisions. It is worthwhile to step back and examine this concept of decision making before we plunge in to build a framework to support it.

Meta-Level Decision Science, as it relates to the way humans make decisions in general, is far too high a level at which to start, instead we will take a cue from the world of finance and use that as a context within which to begin. In managerial finance, the core of what is considered to be the decision making process is referred to as micro-normative, which is defined as a process where a decision maker is selecting between alternative courses of action under uncertainty (probability) while seeking to maximize some objective function (utility theory). This process is carried out in the context of a causal model, which explicitly or implicitly infers causal relationships or links between observable and unobservable aspects of the real world system against which the model is built. We will refer to the combination of models, measures, metrics, and methodologies used to help support the decision maker as a framework. Let's examine each of these in turn.

Decision maker. While this may seem intuitive, it is important to understand that identification of the decision maker(s) is critical to building effective decision support tools and that different decision makers may, and usually will, have different perspectives and requirements. There are literally thousands of decisions made daily in most modern organizations where the process has become much more diffused and decentralized over the past few decades, as the idea of having decisions made by those with a vested interest in the outcome has gained momentum. This decentralization has profound implications for decision support.

Framework. What is a framework? For our purposes here, it is defined as a collection of measures, methodologies, tools, models, and guidelines organized to facilitate meaningful and informed decision making. Typical discussions of framework development in Human Capital Management (HCM) analytics generally start by focusing on the measures (metrics) immediately. "What makes a good metric" is often the place where practitioners attempt to start. This bottom-up approach is starting from the wrong end. The value of a particular metric cannot be determined without knowing the decisions that need to be made. A single metric will often be applicable across a variety of decision processes. The place to start is with the decision itself.

Model. Central to the journey of advancing from simple anecdotal evidence, based on past observations, to a useful framework that allows for prediction of potential future outcomes, is the use of a model. In technical terms, a model is a selective abstraction of a real world system, optimally with enough detail to make it possible to gain an understanding of the real world and test alternatives working with the model. Building a model involves the process of capturing selected characteristics of the real world system and the processes it encompasses, and then combining these into an abstract representation of the original. As long as the model is a reasonably accurate representation, conclusions drawn from such an analysis may be validly extrapolated back to the original system. While this description may make modeling sound formidable, in reality it is the very process that humans go through whenever they are trying to understand any complex system.

It is the complexity of the real world system in its entirety that makes it necessary to develop these abstractions. The model is dependent on the perspective from which it is developed and viewed. My model of an automobile is abstracted from the point of view of the driver interested in getting from point A to point B and is very different from the model that my mechanic utilizes in his daily job of maintaining vehicles. We will be describing techniques where modeling involves defining inputs, entities, actions (including interactions), links, effects, and outcomes. It is these last three items that become the most critical in our development of models. How does a particular action by a particular entity within the system relate to effects upon another entity, cascading through other effects and ultimately manifesting as an outcome?

Take as a simple example a model of the cause and effect relationships related to employee tenure. We'll start with a basic question, "Does salary have an effect on employee tenure?" We may already have a pretty good idea that it does and can move to a hypothesis: "Higher pay in a given job category will lead to longer tenure." Inherent in that hypothesis are a number of potential courses of action, themselves related to making a decision about increasing pay levels in a particular job category. One of the critical relationships in this model is between pay and tenure, which we believe is a causal link.

Causality. The concept of cause and effect is inherent in the way humans understand the workings of everything around them. The ability to relate input factors related to outcome effects is central to building a framework, and being able to predict ahead of time what may happen. Haig Nalbantian and his colleagues at Mercer Human Resources Consulting provide a useful description of the continuum from observed "fact" to "predictable outcome" as it relates to human capital metrics and analytics. Without well understood causal relationships, the task of measuring and interpreting metrics would be essentially pointless as only those measures that were direct would be of any value. The vast majority of the time we are looking to equate the change in one measure with that of another in a cause and effect precedence relationship.

Courses of action. In general, the result of a decision is translated into taking a specific action. In this definition there is no such thing as not deciding or not acting. After all, in any given situation one of the alternatives is to continue the status quo. While this may seem like not deciding, it is choosing a particular course of action. Courses of action generally have definable subcomponents, which may be distinguished as mutually exclusive between different courses. Simply stated, this is when we say, "we can do A or B, but not both." Other situations involve overlapping subcomponents as in "We can do A and B, or A and C." The process of decision making generally involves weighing the alternative courses of action and choosing among them based on the optimization of some objective function.

Utility theory/objective function. Central to the concept of utility theory is the objective function. The objective function embodies the quantification of the goal we are attempting to achieve. Examples include employee retention, return on investment, profit, shareholder value, and so on. Through our causal modeling process we can determine the relationships between what we can control (such as salary, working conditions) and the components of the objective function that we are trying to maximize. If it were as simple as discerning and quantifying the relationships and building the equations, the process of making the decision would be mathematical and could be carried out easily. Unfortunately, it is far from that simple. Identifying, much less quantifying, the linkages in our model is difficult to do within reasonable levels of certainty. One seldom knows exactly what is going on, and it is that uncertainty that is usually the crux of the decision making process.

Uncertainty. A typical dictionary definition of uncertainty is "The condition of being uncertain; doubt." Meaningful decisions are almost always in situations where one is not certain of the outcome; we never have access to the whole truth about our environment. An effective decision making process, and therefore any supporting tools or frameworks, must explicitly deal with this uncertainty.

In the end, decision making comes down to making choices between uncertain outcomes based on partial data from an abstraction of the system that does not provide complete information.

Three Decision Maker Perspectives

Financial management as a decision science has developed a number of frameworks to support these various perspectives in the way most appropriate to each. If left to sift through reams of low level accounting figures, none of these decision makers would get very far. However no single metric or decision framework around a metric could ever be used to serve all decision makers when it comes to financial analysis. This multiple viewpoint and decision support requirement aspect is another important point of comparison between the science of financial analysis, and the emerging science of decision support in HCM.

Consider a large diversified public company and three different decision makers who are engaged in choosing among alternative actions based, to some extent, on financial information. The first decision maker is external to the organization and is deciding whether or not to purchase shares of common stock in the company. As a sophisticated investor, this individual is interested in a variety of important measures related to the financial stability of the company he is interested in investing in. There are literally dozens of metrics that this investor could examine, both at their current values and in the form of trends over time. Many of these metrics would involve ratios of asset and debt figures from the firm's balance sheet and profit and loss statement (the well known "quick ratio" would be a good example). These fairly simple ratios combine two or more accounting level figures, which by themselves have little value. It is critical to know what they were six months ago; two years ago. What is a "good" value for a quick ratio? What are the values for the firm's competitors, in similar but noncompeting industries? The framework of decision support around determining the stability of the financial health of a firm from an asset investment perspective involves more than just the numbers; it includes guiding principles for interpretation and comparison on an intra- and inter-company basis. Once the calculations are defined and understood, the mechanics of the math are relatively simple. The methodology for interpretation, the core of any financial decision framework, is where the complexity and true value inherent in the process emerge.

Let us examine another perspective, this time an internal one; that of the company's Director of Fleet Vehicle Management. It is this person's job to acquire and maintain all of the company's vehicles. In deciding which vehicles (assets) to acquire, this decision maker must examine a large number of metrics. What is the vehicle's capacity, its expected useful life? What mileage does it get? What is the acquisition cost? What are the typical maintenance costs? Once the assets (vehicles) are acquired, how often should they be maintained? Will changing the oil twice as often as the manufacturer suggests lead to longer vehicle life above and beyond the additional costs of the increased maintenance? Here again the decision science of financial management offers a range of metrics and tools to be used along with some guiding principles in making decisions about acquiring assets and optimizing their value (in this case, the vehicle maintenance schedule would have a decided effect on the value of the assets).

An important realization is that neither of these decision makers has been in the Finance department; one is not even part of the firm! Finance and Accounting have provided the tools, metrics, methodologies, and the framework for others to make critical decisions. Thirty years ago it was likely that the decision as to which vehicles to acquire would have been made by someone in Finance. Over the past several decades, the trend has been for Finance to become a supporting role to other departments, disseminating the tools and information to those who should be making the decisions: the ones closest to the action.

Now let's turn to a third perspective, that of the Director of Call Center Operations. The firm currently has an in-house call center that provides phone support for users of the firm's products (their principal business is consumer electronics manufacture, distribution, and sales). The call center employs more than 500 employees in about a dozen locations. Employee turnover is high in this group (as it is in most call centers), and more than a thousand employees come and go in a typical year's time. The firm's product family is large and complex and these products are sold around the globe. Running this call center is a complex task involving critical decision making.

Decisions that the director makes have a significant effect on the operation of the center and, as one of the more significant cost components, on the financial bottom line of the entire company. The director has considerable experience using highly sophisticated tools for making a variety of these decisions. The field of Operations Research, through the use of Queuing Theory, has provided cutting edge tools that allow the director to tune the mechanical aspects of the operation (the number of agents necessary to handle given peak volumes of calls with a predetermined maximum on-hold time as an example) and plan for various contingencies with a fairly high degree of precision. As such the director is not shy when it comes to complexity and the use of tools and models.

Recently, the director has been talking to the Manager of Training, who oversees all personnel training in the organization, including that of employees in the call center. The Manager of Training is suggesting that the current training class, which all new call center employees go through before they start working, be upgraded and expanded from 24 to 32 hours. The hope is that the additional training will provide added value above and beyond the direct costs (training staff and materials) and indirect costs (eight hours less potential productive work from each new employee). The Manager of Training has been investigating this issue based on some information received from Human Resources on exit surveys. It appears that many of the employees, those who leave within the first 90 days of employment, cite a lack of training as one of the reasons they are leaving. Without enough up-front training before they start their new job, many are overwhelmed by the complexity and never feel comfortable.

The director also knows that recent statistics measuring customer satisfaction have shown a marked slip. As part of its customer satisfaction efforts, the firm has been conducting satisfaction surveys within a variety of customer groups, including those who have called in for support. The company has added several new products, one of which is an MP3 player that requires more knowledge on the part of users as well as any support staff with whom they communicate. From their own measures, the director also knows that call handling times appear to be increasing and that the quality scores based on random test call-ins have been declining. On the surface it sounds like additional training may be one component of a solution. However, this will be a fairly expensive proposition. What value will it bring? Will the staff in the call center provide better support? Will they stay on the job longer? If so, what is the value of having them stay longer? How long are they staying now?

These questions sound similar to those that many decision makers face when making choices among alternatives that have differing financial implications in that they relate to investment and return. Unfortunately, the team in Finance does not have a model for helping the director to make this decision. Why not? This seems to fundamentally be an investment optimization problem. The employees in question are certainly critical assets to the company, requiring an up-front investment to acquire and ongoing investments to retain. The knowledge and skills that these employees possess define the very concept of human capital, but where is the framework for understanding the value of this critical component of a firm's asset base? The decisions that affect the optimization of human capital occur throughout the organization. The example above involves only the call center and the training department.

The Role of Human Resources in Decision Support

As with the third example in the previous section, in most organizations, especially with the growth of the service economy, there are few decisions that do not involve the employees, and therefore some aspect of human capital, in one way or another. Critical aspects of these decisions hinge upon an understanding of the value of employees and how specific decisions may enhance or reduce that value. Where does the responsibility for providing the tools and expertise to support human capital related decision making rest?

Boudreau and Ramstad have long espoused the position that the framework for valuing human capital and supporting critical decision making involves investment in it. The application of it should be provided by Human Resources, which meshes well with the current call in Human Resources for new and better metrics. However, much of the current hype around metrics and Human Resources focuses on metrics related to the staffing process itself, such as time to hire, cost of hire, and so on. These efforts are intended to show the efficiency of one of the central processes in Human Resources. It makes sense that early efforts to develop important metrics are focused inward. The decisions being supported are those internal to Human Resources (sourcing choices, process improvements), and the approach often seems to be an ongoing effort to justify Human Resources. All of these efforts generally have little visibility to the rest of the organization. This is in sharp contrast to what one sees in other disciplines that have created effective decision science frameworks. The decision support tools and frameworks provided by Finance are of most interest in their use outside of Finance. The Director of Finance spends much less time measuring the efficiency of Finance operations and much more time supporting the decision making of others in the organization. This is not to say that we should not develop and use metrics in an effort to optimize the staffing process. However, when taken as a percentage component of the overall cost realized by a typical organization, staffing is a small portion. There are many human capital related investment decisions outside of the staffing process that have a much larger impact on the firm's financial well being. Felix Barber and Rainer Strack point out in their *Harvard Business Review* article, "The Surprising Economics of a People Business," that:

> The distinct but generally unappreciated economics of people-intensive businesses call not only for different metrics but also for different management practices. For instance, because even slight changes in employee productivity have a significant impact on shareholder returns, "human resource management" is no longer a support function but a core process for line managers. (Barber and Strack 2005, 81)

This clearly articulates the concept that management of human capital is up to the managers closest to the point where these assets are applied, the line managers. Under such a scenario, the role of the Human Resources department is to support the line managers in carrying out their individual roles as Human Resources managers.

CHAPTER

4

Employee Assets and Contribution

I n the past, employees have generally been regarded as a necessary cost of doing business and not as an asset on the company's
balance sheet. As the economy has shifted from that of physical
production to one of service provision, the role of the employee
has taken on greater and greater importance. Many leading companies have few physical assets and the value of those is dwarfed by
the value of their human capital. How do we value human capital
assets? Before starting the development of a model that describes
the value of employees from a human capital or employee asset
model, we start from the larger perspective that an economist
would use to examine the subject.

Human Capital and Production

For the past several decades, macroeconomists and financial analysts have sought to build usable models that describe the many
complex relationships between the inputs and outputs of production. In the 1940s, two brilliant economists, Paul Douglas and

Richard Cobb, developed what has become known as the Cobb-Douglas Production Function. In its simplest form this model can be described by the formula; $Q = F(C, L, T, R)$ where Q, the quantity of output from the system, is a function (F) of the principal input components, Capital (C), Labor (L), Technology (T), and Raw Materials (R).

This function is generally used to describe the trade-offs of the various inputs that can be made while still maintaining the same level of output Q. For those familiar with this approach, these equal output quantities are referred to as Isoquants.

Dr. Jac Fitz-enz, founder of the Saratoga Institute, would point out that of the components described, Labor, the human component is the only one with the inherent ability to generate value. All the other components have, at best, inert potential, and it is the people who leverage that potential. Labor is also the component with the most variability and least predictability, and it is enormously complex to evaluate. As a result, much of what has happened over the past several decades is a drive towards substitution of other factors for Labor, or Human Capital. Much of what is described as the increase in productivity of the U.S. labor force is in fact the result of substitution of other factors for labor. Dramatic improvements in Information Technology (part of the T in the Cobb-Douglas model) have fueled the information revolution over the past 40 years. IT investment has increased at a rate of 7.4 percent per year since 1960, yet the overall output of the economy as measured by Gross National Product (GNP) has increased by only 3 percent per year. The ratio of IT investment to labor cost has grown from 0.4 percent in 1980 to 5.3 percent today. By substituting IT for labor or ordinary capital, organizations seek to capitalize on the vastly superior price and performance improvements in IT relative to other inputs.

Meanwhile, focus on the human component has been limited in terms of building a solid economic and financial theory around the valuation of human capital. When there are other parts of the model that are easier to deal with and offer the potential of huge returns, why deal with the least tangible component—human capital?

As in all forms of incremental improvement with a drive towards optimization, focus will shift and already is doing so. The elasticity of substitution for human capital is, as one would expect, approaching unity and when it drops below that, when we can not substitute for human capital with a less expensive input and maintain the same output, more and more emphasis will be placed on valuing human capital.

Modeling employees as assets is a fairly recent phenomenon, heralded initially by emergence of the term Human Capital. Theodore Schultz, winner of the Nobel Prize in Economics in 1979, originally coined the term Human Capital and defined it in the following manner:

> Consider all human abilities to be either innate or acquired. Every person is born with a particular set of genes, which determines his innate ability. Attributes of acquired population quality, which are valuable and can be augmented by appropriate investment, will be treated as human capital. (Schultz 1981, 21)

A critical concept here is that of "augmentation by appropriate investment." In general, when we are analyzing and attempting to measure Human Capital, it is in the context of making those augmenting investments. In knowing the absolute value of a pool of human capital (that is, your employee population is not of much interest in and of itself), what we are trying to develop is an ability to measure the change in that asset pool as we make various different augmenting investments. Dr. Schultz was ahead of his time back in the 1960s and 1970s, and much of his thinking is still beyond current practice.

Human Capital and Intellectual Capital

Under the pressures brought about by the drive to contain costs and improve competitiveness and efficiency, the role of employees has been reduced to those areas where they cannot be cost effectively substituted. The industrial age dawned with the introduction of labor saving machinery. For simple, repetitive, dangerous, unpleasant tasks, machines quickly replaced human workers. Over time machines replaced humans in ever more complicated tasks such as auto body assembly. Fewer employees are required per auto produced, and those working in the assembly plants have much more complex jobs programming, maintaining, and running the robots and automated systems that actually assemble the cars.

While many jobs have been eliminated through automation, hundreds of new jobs have been developed out of necessity over the past several decades. The vast majority of these are knowledge jobs. In these jobs, employees are paid more for thinking than for physically performing tasks. There is a range in the spectrum of knowledge required for these positions.

Starting at the simpler end, consider the now ubiquitous barista making your favorite caffeinated drink, in my case a 20-ounce, nonfat, half-decaffeinated latte. The office that I work in has a nice kitchen area with a machine that can create a variety of such drinks automatically, and it's free! Yet on Monday, Wednesday, and Friday, a local company brings in one of those traveling barista carts, and the line is long. I much prefer to pay the $3.25 than to drink the free machine-made version. The difference between the two involves the product (the machine cannot make it exactly the way I want) and the service. The barista provides excellent customer service and a better product—enough of a differentiator that a significant number of my colleagues and I opt to pay the extra cost. This same scenario plays out across what many consider the low end, low skill, hourly worker positions. Employees in these positions use knowledge and skills to transform raw materials into product.

At the other extreme of the knowledge work spectrum, the product does not even take physical form directly. Consider positions in the so-called high-knowledge sector such as consulting, where in its purest form the product is know-how. A recent survey by Salary.com concluded that one of the highest paid (lowest on the glamour scale) jobs, is that of tax attorney.

As the knowledge economy grows, knowledge work is quickly replacing physical labor and, with this shift, the knowledge, skills, and experience of people. Human capital is becoming more important than the physical capital which dominated the economy of the past.

Modeling Employee Contribution

Many measurable factors within the work environment have an impact on, or can be related to, employee asset value. Unicru has coined the term Incremental Employee Contribution, or IEC Model, as a label for the model that has been developed to help organizations address key questions that relate to the value of their employees, and to examine alternative interventions aimed at optimizing the asset value of their employee pool. To date, the IEC model has been used successfully to examine relationships among length of service, time to competency, productivity, the value of retention, employee asset value, and, ultimately, employee profitability.

Developing a meaningful framework relating Human Capital to outcomes relevant to an organization on a financial performance basis requires an asset model applicable to that Human Capital. The key concept is the development of an understanding of employees as an asset rather than as an expense.

To illustrate, let's describe a simplified employee asset model applicable to many environments in the service and manufacturing sectors in which employees are paid hourly with a well-defined and understandable set of tasks in their job description. Their role is understood, and their productivity can be measured directly or indirectly. We also have an estimate of the cost of acquisition. This information, including a few assumptions, allows us to build a simple but fairly robust model.

The foundation of the employee asset model, as with any asset-based model, includes the following important concepts:

- An employee asset is acquired at some definable (though not necessarily measurable) cost.

- An employee asset has a measurable life cycle from acquisition to departure. Some employees may return to the same firm several times during their career.

- An employee asset engaged in a process requires inputs in the form of cash or value flows and provides a series of cash or value flows over time in return.

In addition, there are some unique aspects to employee assets that prevent us from simply adapting a fixed asset modeling methodology. Some of these differences include the following:

- The value of an employee asset changes over its lifecycle in ways far more complex than those of typical fixed assets.

- Employees must generally learn the processes in which they are engaged.

- Interactions between employees, their managers, and other aspects of the organization have a profound effect on the value of a particular employee.

- Post–employee acquisition investments in employee assets (training, promotions, and incentives) have a larger relative effect on the value and performance than can be described in the typical fixed asset model.

One way to model employee value is to utilize some of the components and methodologies found in the typical decision support tools used in conventional financial modeling. Two commonly used models are:

- Net Present Value (NPV) Analysis. Related to cash flow analysis, this approach views the cost of acquiring an asset, with inflows and outflows of value supporting the ongoing engagement of that asset in the processes essential to the operation of the organization. Of interest to the valuation of employee assets is the idea of an asset value lifecycle and a methodology that properly accounts for the time value of money. An investment today in today's dollars is offset over time by returns obtained in the future. These returns must be discounted to today's value.

- Temporal Break-Even Analysis. Unit production break-even analysis is a basic principle taught in Finance 101. The idea is to determine how many units of a product, given a known variable cost to produce each unit and known overhead or fixed costs, must be produced to attain break-even status. This unit volume break-even analysis approach observes fixed and variable costs related to a process, operation, or asset life cycle and determines at what volume profitability is attained within a given set of constraints including the cost of capital. Temporal break-even recasts the analysis from a volume basis to one related to time; that is, the time when a process becomes profitable. In this case, the time span we will examine is the employee life cycle. How long must employees be retained before the costs of their acquisition, training, salary, and benefits are paid off? While it sounds simple on paper, the actual practice of making this determination is complex in all but the simplest job categories.

The Incremental Employee Contribution Model

The Incremental Employee Contribution or IEC model combines the concepts described above; a simplified version is described here. Mathematically, the incremental value that an employee provides within the system can be described as:

P_t Potential incremental revenue on day t attributable to this employee.

S_t Salary cost on day t for this employee.

D_t Drag cost on day t.

O_t Allocated overhead cost on day t.

U Total up-front acquisition cost for this employee.

Graphically these relationships are shown in Figure 4.1.

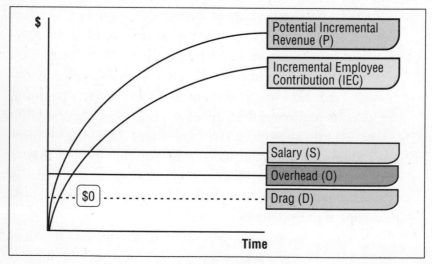

Figure 4.1

Descriptively, this model is a statement of the following inputs, effects, links, and causality.

- The longer employees are on the job, the more productive they become. Learning theory supports this proposition and allows for the quantification of a learning curve, which relates the level of productivity, skill, capacity, or capability to length of time on the job (Teplitz 1991).
- System resources in the form of such things as training materials, additional management oversight, and so on.
- Overhead costs are constant over time.
- Salary stays steady over time.
- The incremental value of an employee is negative on the first day, becomes positive over time, and then eventually levels out at a steady rate of productivity (asymptotic).

Each of these statements involves some implicit or explicit set of assumptions and beliefs. These points are oversimplified for illustration purposes (for example, one would not realistically expect that the salary level would remain constant over time).

Each individual employee tracks to a different trajectory along these curves. However, it is not necessary to quantify the exact trajectory for each and every employee. The goal is to build a robust enough model that allows us to weigh broader issues.

From an asset valuation perspective, an important question becomes, "At what point in time has a new employee broken even in terms of investment?" Alternatively, "What is the payback period?" One detail worth mentioning is the scale of the Y axis. We are not interested in the absolute value of the productive output, but rather the relative value to other employees in the system.

The key concept here is the Fully Effective Employee, one who is up to speed and performing the job within established quality and productivity guidelines. While it may be possible to determine the exact dollar value of production from an employee at a given time (probably only in the simplest job categories), it is not necessary in order to support the decision framework and would require a great deal more work. There will be many situations where we do not know the value of the efforts the employee makes but we do have an idea of their relative productivity.

Using the model, we can accumulate the incremental value over time and account for the initial outlay required to acquire the asset; see Figure 4.2.

This graph of the cumulative IEC shows information that was not easily deduced from either the mathematical model, or the nonaccumulated IEC graph. This is the essence of modeling, abstracting from the real world system to something more cognitively tractable when making our decision. From the graph, the cumulative value of an employee decreases over an initial period and then

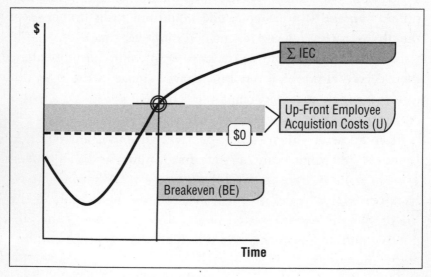

Figure 4.2

increases. At some point it becomes greater than zero and at another it rises above the acquisition cost to achieve break-even status, the date that defines the end of the payback period. The graph also shows that the worst time to lose an employee is at the bottom of that initial trough, the point at which the cumulative value is the lowest.

CHAPTER

5

Employee Contribution to Risk

R isk has been defined as the chance of something happening that will have an impact upon objectives. Risk management is an attitude of mind that should pervade all levels in an organization. It needs to be undertaken on an ongoing basis and in a proactive manner. Without proper risk management, an organization is less likely to achieve its objectives in an efficient and effective way. As firms look to optimize corporate value, the role and need for effective risk management have grown. Of all the organizational factors, the role of the employee in risk impact is among the most complex.

Employees significantly impact the risk profile of a firm, primarily in the category of operational risk, and more specifically in the areas of worker safety and service provision liability. Organizations that are actively seeking to manage risk to an efficient risk frontier can use a number of tools to optimize their risk profile, including the transfer and mitigation of risk. Risk mitigation efforts that focus on current and future employees can return value in the form of reduced costs well beyond the costs incurred in implementing these mitigation efforts. Employee selection should focus on identifying employees who are more likely to work safely, follow processes, and act conscientiously, and are less likely to be negligent, act carelessly, or manifest deviant behaviors such as malingering. This can be a cost effective tool in reducing employee related risk exposure.

Background

The Incremental Employee Contribution model (Chapter 4) provides an analytical framework for the analysis of employee value from the point of view of positive contribution associated with productivity, time to competency, and other factors. While providing positive value to the organization, employees also impact the organization in a number of areas not directly tied to productivity, most critically in the areas of risk and loss. The term risk is used here in the context of describing potential harm or loss.

The current trend in risk management is toward the development of an integrated framework for describing and discussing various aspects of risk with the goal of quantifying a risk profile, or portfolio of risks. This quantification is carried out in an effort to establish the total impact of risk and loss for an organization. Commonly referred to as Enterprise Risk Management or ERM (deLoach, 2000), modern risk management is focused on understanding the sources of risk from multiple perspectives. Under the ERM framework a risk exists if:

- It is specifically definable as an observable event or action that can have a material impact on the financial or operational performance of an organization.
- It is measurable using a standard unit of account (such as revenues, percentage of return, EBIT, etc.).
- It is observable over a period of time.

Organizations are moving from a paradigm where controls were the focus and action was generally discontinuous and after the fact, to one where the keys are:

- Avoid/diversify risk.
- Share/transfer risk.
- Control/accept risk.

One of the core tenets of ERM is that risk is capital with both downside potential and upside or profitability characteristics. An organization that can more effectively identify and manage its portfolio of risks can establish an advantage over its competitors by exploiting its superior risk management approach. In this new ERM paradigm, organizations seek to understand their risk portfolio or risk profile. The process of developing a risk profile is generally known as risk assessment. In discussing how employees impact an organization's risk profile, it is useful to use a framework familiar to those who analyze risk, its sources, and costs, as the prime focus of their work.

Categorizing Risks—Type and Source

Risks do not occur in isolation and can generally be grouped and allocated to categories or domains. In the ERM framework, risks can be can be allocated to one or more of several categories (Walker, Shenkir, and Barton 2002).

Hazard Risk: Risks that are insurable, such as natural disasters; various insurable liabilities; impairment of physical assets; terrorism.

Financial Risk: Risks associated with an organization's ability to raise capital, maintain access to capital, and contracting issues.

Strategic Risk: This category includes risks that impact the growth of an organization. Examples include risks related to strategy, political, economic, regulatory, and global market conditions; it could also include leadership risk, brand risk, and changing customer needs. This category also includes reputation risks that center on performance expectations related to customer and community relations.

Human Capital Risk: Risks associated with the acquisition, management, and maintenance of a human workforce. These risks include worker compensation, unionization, turnover, absenteeism, strikes, workplace violence, harassment, and discrimination. Environmental issues related to safety and security, plus occupational and environmental hazards, are also included in this category.

Operational Risk: Risks related to an organization's systems, processes, technology, and people. This is risk associated with the operation of the business itself, including those associated with the processes and people in the organization responsible for the operations. Outside of the category specific to human capital risk, employees also have a significant impact on an organization's risk profile through their contribution to operational risk.

Legal and Regulatory Risk: Risks associated with a range of corporate, legal, and regulatory compliance issues.

Technology Risk: This category includes risks associated with the use of new technology in the operations or management of an organization, or as part of the product or service offered.

These categories are meant as a way of organizing risks. When looking at a particular component of an organization, the associated risks may fall into more than one category. For example, risks associated with employees fall into the categories of operational risk, human capital risk, and legal and regulatory risk.

Table 5.1

Severity	Frequency
Low Frequency High Severity	High Frequency High Severity
Low Frequency Low Severity	High Frequency Low Severity

Categorizing Risks—Frequency and Consequence

Knowing the sources of risk in an organization is important. However, in order to focus efforts for maximum benefit, it is necessary
to understand two key factors. Specifically: 1) how often will the
risk manifest as an actual loss, and 2) what is the severity or consequence of that loss? Table 5.1 places the possible combinations into
risk quadrants.

Most organizations initially focus on the upper right-hand quad-
rant, where small incremental reductions in risk exposure can have
a large impact on the value of the organization.

Categorizing Costs

There are costs associated with risk and loss, some components of
which are more measurable than others. In developing a framework with which to measure and predict these costs it is useful to
allocate them as follows:

Risk Transfer Costs: Insurance is the most common way in which
organizations transfer operational risks. Various hedging strategies
are used to transfer certain forms of financial risk. For example, a
firm with a significant exposure to foreign currency rate volatility
may choose to purchase various currency related options in an effort
to offset the negative impacts of changes in exchange rates.

Risk Mitigation Costs: Organizations undertake, at a cost, a variety of programs in an effort to reduce the probability of a negative event occurrence and thus reduce the risk profile in a given area. There are three general components of most risk mitigation plans in regards to employees: training, job/equipment design, and employee selection.

Direct Loss Costs: When negative events do occur, there are often direct costs related to them, costs not covered by insurance payments. An example would be the deductible a company has to pay in order to cover the first dollars of cost for repair incurred due to an accident.

Indirect Loss Costs: Incidents related to operational risks often impose indirect costs far beyond those that are directly attributable to the incident itself. For example, after a work related accident, an employee's absence requires that other employees work overtime to cover for the reduction in capacity. The cost of overtime would be an indirect cost related to the injured employee's accident.

Quantifying the Risk Profile

Using the framework described here, it is possible to quantify a risk profile for an organization. For a given risk profile, it is then possible to project expected costs under a set of assumptions. It is also possible to alter a firm's risk profile. For example, additional risk can be transferred by obtaining additional insurance, or insurance with lower deductibles; however, the costs associated with making that shift may outweigh the reduction in costs associated with the new risk profile itself. This leads to the idea of an efficient risk frontier (Friedel 2001), which defines the optimal combination of risk retained, risk transferred, and risk mitigated or avoided that is most cost effective for a projected set of circumstances. The frontier shifts as expectations of future conditions change. Organizations, for which risk management is critical, often use complex scenario analysis methodologies to test various risk frontiers under differing sets of assumptions and conditions.

Quantifying Return

Even without going into a significant level of detail, an organization can come to understand the trade-offs in expected costs and returns arising from different interventions and programs aimed at altering an organization's risk profile. Rather than attempting to evaluate the absolute cost of any particular scenario, it is only necessary to consider incremental change, such as what will the increase/decrease in costs be if a particular approach is taken.

With the preceding as background, the focus now shifts to an examination of how employees impact, directly and indirectly, the risk profile and associated costs. As mentioned earlier, most of the risk attributable to employees falls into two categories: strategic risk and operational risk. A number of subcomponents relevant to strategic risk hinge upon an organization's ability to attract and retain qualified employees in order to fulfill its strategic objectives. While the employee impact on strategic risk is critical, the focus here will be on operational risk, in particular two subcategories: worker safety risk and service provision related liability risk. A third area of employee related risk not covered in this discussion is product shrinkage or loss.

Worker Safety Related Risk. In virtually any operation involving employees, there are accidents. The consequence of these accidents is manifested in a variety of ways. An employee who is injured on the job causes the organization to incur costs ranging from payments made for treatment and missed time to the costs of additional overtime necessary to cover production for a missing worker.

Risk Transfer Costs. Worker's Compensation Insurance, a mandatory program for virtually all business firms in the United

States, allows an organization to transfer some of the risks associated with workplace accidents to a third party. This third party then makes some of the payments that the firm would otherwise be directly obligated to pay. Worker's Compensation Insurance is a complex subject in and of itself and the discussion here is not inclusive but touches on a few key points relating to costs. As with other forms of insurance, there are costs associated with this risk transfer in the form of premium payments. The cost of transferring worker safety risk depends on the loss experience of the organization. In 1995 there were more than 3.6 million disabling accidents in the U.S. workplace. In that year, firms paid more than $30 billion in Worker's Compensation premiums, representing the largest component of the $131 billion in commercial liability premiums paid (Lencsis 1998, 1). Two companies, otherwise identical, will pay different premiums based on the rate of claims over the past several years. Claims rate experience from the previous four years (three years of actual rates with a one year lag to compensate for open claims) is a common approach for setting the rates differentially from a baseline for a given industry. Logically, companies that have experienced higher rates of claims must pay a higher cost to transfer the risk associated with potential future claims. Because of the lag in resetting rates based on experience, firms that reduce their claims rates generally must wait a year or more before they start to see reduced premiums for Worker's Compensation Insurance.

Loss Costs. When a worker is injured on the job, there are a variety of directly and indirectly associated costs not covered by insurance payouts. It may be necessary to increase overtime for remaining employees in order to cover for absent employees. This is especially true in environments where there is little spare capacity, which is common with the current drive toward efficient staffing and in environments where there is a lack of qualified employees. Product or service quality may suffer due to the absence of an employee. Production schedules may slip. Organizations that are part of a supply chain can see effects ripple throughout the system.

Costs associated with simply processing and following up on claims can accumulate to surprising levels. Employees who are injured, but still on the job, require additional management resources. Many of the indirect loss costs are difficult to accurately quantify, but it is useful for an organization to enumerate them and explore their potential impact.

Risk Mitigation Costs. Organizations employ a variety of approaches in attempts to reduce workplace accidents, ranging from system safety (making sure that the equipment and processes in place are optimized from the point of view of safe operations with cost constraints) to employee selection and training.

As there are costs associated with any mitigation efforts, it is critical to prioritize those likely to have the most impact. Job Safety Analysis (JSA) provides a high level description of the work environment from the point of view of discovering causes of accidents. People, processes, and equipment interact in a complex system that can and does lead to accidents. The process and equipment components can lead to unsafe conditions, whereas the people (employees) engage in unsafe acts. Ultimately the intersection of unsafe acts and unsafe conditions is where accidents can occur (Wert and Bryan 2001, 45). In some environments, such as manufacturing, a great deal of work has been done to reduce the impact of unsafe conditions. In a recent study, DuPont found that only 4 percent of accidents were due to faulty equipment or other technical issues. The other 96 percent could be attributed to unsafe acts by employees (Olin 2003). Much of this study was based on data from manufacturing environments where firms like DuPont have a long history of aggressively improving safety issues related to physical systems technology. This would suggest that mitigation efforts may best be effectively leveraged when they are structured around employees, in particular the selection of new employees.

Service Liability Risk Related. Liability risk, within operational risk, covers a range of issues. Here the concentration is upon liability risk associated with the provision of service. In environments where there is direct or indirect interaction between the firm's employees and its customers, there is the potential for adverse impact on the customer, and this impact can often be traced to a particular incident, which can itself be related to the actions of employees. For example, a shopper in a grocery store slips and falls on a recently mopped floor where no caution sign was displayed to warn the customers. The shopper is injured and the store faces a potential liability claim. Some service environments have much larger liability risk potential than others. Healthcare is an excellent example, where the costs of shifting liability risks to third parties as well as the costs of losses are very high (Carroll 2004).

Healthcare liability issues as they relate to the nation's medical liability system are a prominent issue today both economically and politically. Patient safety issues can be, to a significant extent, attributed to actions of the employees of the healthcare firms. The Joint Commission on Accreditation of Healthcare Organizations (JCAHO), one of several oversight groups in a complex system, is responsible for accrediting healthcare organizations and ensuring high quality patient care and patient safety. The JCAHO recognizes the link between patient safety, liability costs (both loss and risk transfer costs), and healthcare organization employees (JCAHO, 2005)

Risk Transfer Costs. Liability insurance is the most common form of risk transfer. Premium rates are dependent upon the type of business and the previous loss experience, which is considered to be a predictor of future risk potential. The liability insurance market has seen a significant hardening in recent years due to a generally perceived increase in risk across nearly all sectors of business, coupled with a recent increase in estimated hazard risks. The healthcare industry, in particular, has seen a dramatic rise in the costs of transferring risk; The industry is at the point where the costs of doing this may become so prohibitive that it is not possible to continue operations. These spiraling costs threaten to cripple the industry (Joint Commission on Accreditation of Healthcare Organizations 2005a and b).

Loss Costs. In the context of liability related losses, costs are incurred to pay for the portion of risk not transferred (deductibles being a good example) as well as other indirect loss costs. Liability related lawsuits for wrongful damages incurred by customers are becoming more and more prevalent in most business sectors, and firms assume significant risk of loss not covered by their liability policies. Liability issues also impose a variety of indirect costs. A firm's reputation may be diminished in the case of extreme liability issues (Firestone Tire being a prime example), which has an effect on future revenue potentials. In some cases there exist complex indirect causality relationships. Again in healthcare, the JCAHO accredits healthcare organizations based on a complex set of rules and guidelines. The consequence of failing the accreditation process can be drastic, as eligibility for a variety of payment systems like Medicare and participation in healthcare insurance networks are tied to continued accreditation. Healthcare organizations that experience patient safety issues consequently face higher risk transfer costs in the future, higher current loss costs in the present, and an increased probability of a catastrophic loss of accreditation. The loss of accreditation is an example of a very low frequency occurrence but with very high consequences, which is in turn driven by an aggregation of higher frequency individual incidents, each with lower direct consequences.

Risk Mitigation Costs. As with worker safety related risks, firms engage in a wide variety of efforts in an attempt to mitigate liability risk. In service oriented environments, the most cost effective programs will be those that focus on the employee, through training of current employees and selection of future employees.

6

The Employee Lifecycle— A Metrics Roadmap from the C-Level

In a 2006 HRMetrics.org survey of C-level executives, managers were asked to identify, in ranked order, the most important metrics to them within performance and HR. What's not surprising in the result of the survey looks different than the dashboard report that many HR teams probably present to executives. What was surprising was not that HR and other C-level executives were misaligned in what kind of data they thought was important, or that HR had no clear set of value propositions for executives to review. It was that executives and HR intuitively understood those measures that were important to them, and while other metrics might not be important to them, they are important to some other part of the organization.

The metrics that executives favored over others are likely the ones that ideally would be on an executive HR dashboard. Does your HR dashboard have different metrics than what the C-level wants to see? Some of their wishes are difficult to measure (or at least, the cost of measuring it is greater than the benefit of having it), and some may not have an established metric at all to it. Sometimes, however, it is measurable, and we just don't know how to use the data.

Managing Through Metrics

Metrics have the ability to change the business processes of an entire company overnight. Companies that have embraced any quality program (Six Sigma, etc.) can attest to the power of a good metric. But what makes a quality metric powerful is that it's directed towards a process. A Six Sigma is meaningless unless it is directed to measure something you suspect needs to be managed or changed. How many metrics have been created because the data is available and you need something for the big executive meeting that looks good on a pie chart?

Building metrics throughout the talent life cycle must have a management goal. It does not need to be an executive goal, but there must be an intended audience, a management or change goal, and a buy-in on that goal by all stakeholders.

An example of using a powerful metric the wrong way: At a recent conference on metrics, an HR manager complained that their hiring manager's contracted time-to-fill metric, which is an agreed time-to-fill service level between recruiter and hiring manager, hadn't impacted the time-to-fill of recruiting at all. Probing further we discovered that hiring managers set the date for time-to-fill without any HR agreement. Literally, in this contracted time-to-fill, one of the parties (HR) had no say in setting the measure! There is no possible way a change can occur if the teams working in the process can't both agree to participate in change management.

When it comes to leveraging change using HR metrics, it may

be helpful to categorize the metric according to the audience to confirm you are using the right metric for the right audience. A simple categorization of HR metrics according to audience is as follows:

Managing Up. Metrics that are meant to satisfy objectives that HR and executive teams have agreed will impact larger business objectives. If your metric is managing some priority up the management chain, it's important that your team and the executive teams understand what you want to measure to.

Managing Out. Metrics can also leverage change within the constituents that you serve. HR can leverage change with hiring managers to reduce time-to-fill, to increase retention rates of "A" players, to improve the interviewing experience, and much more. These metrics support the improvement of talent metrics.

Managing Down. These metrics are likely the most frequently used within HR that optimize the performance of the HR and recruiting teams themselves. These metrics have interest to managers within HR and to those that are being measured, but have little interest outside of the HR organization.

Once you categorize the metric, it becomes clear what metrics you want to present to an audience and which ones you may not. How many times have executive eyes glazed over when reviewing a source of hire chart for the Q1 recruiting cycle?

The Chief Human Resources Officer (CHRO) versus Other C-Level Executives

The 2006 HRMetrics.org survey of C-level executives helps to illustrate the difference between the tools that HR needs to manage their teams versus what other C-level executives want to see from HR.

When asked which metrics are most important to each group in

Table 6.1

	CHRO	Other C-Level
1	HR Employee to Total Employee Ratio	New Hire Quality
2	Cost-per-Hire	Line Manager Satisfaction
3	Time-to-Fill	Recruiting Efficiency Ratio
4	Vacancy Rate	Time-to-Start
5	Turnover Ratio	Vacancy Rate

the survey (CHRO and other C-level executives), their top five metrics look like those show in Table 6.1.

The CHRO and other C-level managers share only one metric in their top five metrics. Does this mean that HR is just wrong and they are not aligned with the business? Of course not. What it does mean is that the CHRO is responsible for not only managing up to the executive team, but also down to their staff and out to their constituents. The CHRO top five list is far more spread out against the three audiences that they are responsible for managing. And that's the key to solving a core problem in presenting to executive management: Many times the CHRO is presenting the wrong metrics to the executive audience.

Metrics to manage the executive team are notoriously difficult. Shifting priorities, business decisions, and the events of a quarter will impact what piques the interest of executives on any given day. However, when the entire list of metrics in order of importance is reviewed, the list evens out considerably—both executives and CHROs intuitively understand the metrics that are important for different audiences. The results from the survey are shown in Table 6.2 and demonstrate the combined understanding.

There are literally hundreds of metrics documented as best practices by the Saratoga Institute, HR consulting organizations, the Society of Human Resources Management (SHRM), and

Table 6.2

Metrics Ratings	CHROs	Other C-Level
New Hire Quality	7.7	9.6
Line Manager Satisfaction	7.4	9.3
Recruiting Efficiency Ratio	7.8	8.9
Time-to-Start	7.2	8.6
Vacancy Rate	8.5	8.4
Turnover Ratio	7.9	8.2
Actual/Contracted Time to Start	6.2	8.1
HR Expense to Operating Expense	5.6	7.4
HR Expense per Employee	5.8	7.3
Revenue per Employee	6.1	7.3
Net Income per Employee	6.2	6.8
Cost-per-Hire	8.6	6.7
Quality of Candidate	7.1	6.4
Salaries as a percentage of operating income	5.9	6.4
HR Employee to Total Employee Ratio	9.3	6.2
Time-to-Fill	8.6	6.2
Health Care Expense per Covered Employee	6.2	6.1
Health Care Expense per Employee	5.9	5.8
Health Care Expense Increase	5.9	5.5
Annual Salary Increase	5.8	5.0

HRMetrics.org. Here we provide a high-level overview of helpful metrics through each part of the lifecycle, using the most highly rated metrics from the survey with some other common metrics. We will categorize the metrics by their likely audience as well. The talent lifecycle categories we will use are as follows:

Attract → Acquire → Develop → Utilize → Separate

Attract

This pertains to all metrics relating to sourcing, brand-awareness, the candidate pipeline, optimizing candidate attraction budgets, and sources.

Managing Up. Executives most want to understand the relative costs of attracting talent to the organization using statistics. Examples include the recruiting cost ratio and the overall staffing situation as it stands right now using vacancy rate data, since there is a direct link between vacancy rate and revenue in many organizations.

Managing Out. Using metrics to manage hiring manager behavior in the "attract" stage of talent development to focus in on metrics helps assess the interest level in hiring managers to attract high quality talent. The end result of this can include frequency of referring candidates for positions, feedback on sourcing strategies, and even participation in hiring events at colleges and so on. Used in this way, metrics can illustrate top management performers in acquiring new talent.

Managing Down. Managing the recruiting function in attracting candidates may range from the simple (total number of applicants/month, basic source per hire, percentage sourced from agencies) to the complex (detailed source effectiveness, employment brand awareness surveys, and qualified candidates per requisition, and the recruiter cost ratio). In managing down, using outside comparative data from SHRM, Staffing.org, HRMetrics.org, or even against your own benchmarks will help the internal organization. Keep in mind that these metrics are really only interesting to the HR team! An example of benchmark data on sources per hire is a Media Tracker report that uses standard advertising metrics applied to talent. Developed by the author, this metric shows benchmark data of job posting performance on several job boards against industry data. See Figure 6.1.

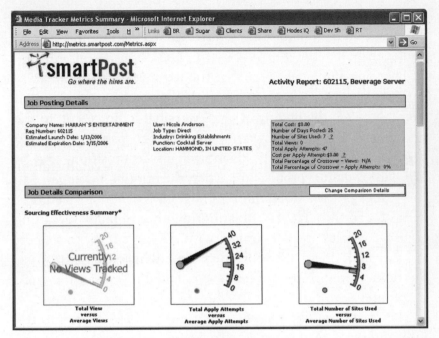

Figure 6.1

Two other areas of measurement for the recruiting team to consider are specific measures for employee referral programs (time to contact, top referrers) and diversity recruiting measures.

Acquire

This refers to all tasks relating to screening, assessing, interviewing, offering, and hiring candidates into open jobs.

Managing Up. Interestingly, two of the top five C-level metrics fall under this phase of the lifecycle: new hire quality and time-to-start. Careful readers have already noted that executives did not report the time-to-fill metric (almost always using the hire/offer accept date) as important. Executives want to see the time it takes for the candidate to start working at the company. The time-to-fill number is interesting to HR, but not to this audience.

That new hire quality rated as the top metric that executives care about is both exciting and problematic. It is exciting that executives feel the quality of employees has a direct link to the performance indicators that they are tasked to manage (financial performance, competitive advantage, market position, and so on). However, it is problematic when the priority is compared to the reality of the HR/recruiting budget. As a senior vice president of a Fortune 100 HR organization once noted, "Recruiting is just like Sales and Marketing, with a lousy budget to support it." Certainly there is opportunity for HR management to use metrics to leverage the investment required to impact the quality of hire.

Managing Out. There is the opportunity to use metrics as the measuring stick for the service level agreement between HR and the Hiring Manager. In acquiring talent, the metric that was most consistently a sore point in between recruiting and their constituents is Contracted Time to Fill. Note that this is a contract for a service level of both parties, HR and Hiring Manager alike. There is little chance that a contracted time to fill can be improved without both parties creating the service level. At a recent HR Metrics conference, we found several HR analysts frustrated that while they've implemented the contracted time to fill metric, their number had not decreased at all in months. After drilling down further we found that the Hiring Manager was dictating the time to fill date, regardless of their recruiter's feedback on the reality of recruiting that position, in that market, and/or at that salary level. Using contracted time to fill as a true partnership has a much higher likelihood of leveraging change than without it.

Another helpful weapon in managing hiring managers is the

Hiring Manager Time-to-Respond metric, which has been used in many organizations to illustrate how quickly a hiring manager is able to get back to the recruiter with feedback on resumes supplied for their jobs. This can be a power motivator when the hiring manager can see the ranked order of their performance against their peers, knowing that their managers also see this data.

Managing Down. Managing the recruiting function in acquiring talent is probably the most clearly documented segment of recruiting metrics available, so we will not drill down deeply here. However, note that the Recruiting Efficiency Ratio is not just a powerful tool for executives, it is a tool for HR to understand how they perform against their peers in other organizations. Recruiters are remarkable people—and competitive too! Great recruiters want to beat out their competition for talent, and they want to do it faster and better. Comparative metrics (hires per recruiter, talent pipeline metrics, and so on) within the recruiting team are usually readily available from the company Applicant Tracking System (ATS) as well. Maximize the data that you have here.

Bad Data Starts with Bad Process. The top 20 or so talent management systems are far more advanced than the applicant tracking systems of years ago. It used to be a burden for recruiters to status candidates inside of their system—no recruiter wanted to do it. Not so with today's systems. Recruiters benefit from using these systems in myriad ways from better search and resume data mining, to keeping talent pools of data and automated offer letters. The price for recruiters within your organization should be meticulous interview statusing. With newer systems, it takes seconds to status batches of candidates at a time. And it gives the HR analyst who is running metrics the data needed to create many of the reports that you need. If you have a good process and enforcement, good data will come naturally.

Develop

Metrics associated with development include ways to measure training, professional learning, education, and promoting.

Managing Up. Interestingly, C-level executives rated understanding learning and development (L&D) metrics higher than the HR executive did in the survey. There is interest in how the L&D role impacts the organization. What processes have been streamlined through training? What elements of worker safety training have helped decline an injury rate? Has employee feedback on their managers improved since the last set of management training? In knowledge-based organizations, percentage of revenue spent on training is a huge element in assessing the investment in new intellectual capital for consultants.

Managing Out. Average Time to Break-even on Employee Contribution can be a helpful measurement coming out of learning and development that may provide insight into new ways to accelerate the process of getting an employee productive faster within a ramp-up time. Identifying and measuring those key processes become even more essential if your organization depends heavily on freelance, temp, and other workers that need to understand your needs and your culture without taking months to do so.

Managing Down. There are many indirect measures for developing employees that focus on including the percentage of Internal Hires, Employee Fluidity, Measuring Internal Mobility by A,B,C players, and more.

Utilize

This refers to all aspects of employee productivity.

Managing Up. In a separate Staffing.org survey with the same audience, high on the executives' list of metrics is the health and safety of their employees. These are great metrics, even if your organization is not involved in risky enterprises in industrial manufacturing, mining, and so on. The less time staff is out sick, the more work gets done. It's apparent in the survey that there is a genuine interest in the welfare of the staff the executives are responsible for.

Managing Out: Human Resources has some talent optimization weapons that can be used to manage Hiring Managers proactively. Trends on internal transfer requests can be real-time indicators of issues between a manager and one or more employees. We know the rule of thumb that employees join companies and leave their managers. By watching the trends on internal transfers, HR has the opportunity to directly probe and intervene on the management level to improve a situation, recommend management training, and ultimately decrease voluntary turnover.

Managing Down: In managing the development process, learning and development and performance management tools become the source of metrics—and the place where one can extract interesting information that pertains to managing the HR function better. Process improvement measures are helpful here, as well as are compensation and competitiveness, internal mobility, and HR time to contact measures.

The top six highest priority topics according to C-level executives are shown in Table 6.3.

Table 6.3

Metric Priorities	C-level	CHROs
Health and Safety	9.7	8.5
Organization Readiness	9.5	7.0
New Hire Quality	9.4	8.6
Worker [and Work Group] Performance	9.1	7.2
Employee [Assessment and] Performance	8.9	7.4
Employee Development	8.8	8.2

Separate

This refers to all metrics that track employee turnover and retention rates.

Managing Up. One would expect that the turnover rate would be the key number that HR and executives point to on separation, and it does top the list in this category. However, other data such as the cost of vacancy are interesting as well when accompanied by an action plan.

Managing Out. One of the most useful bits of data to compile over long periods of time is turnover rates per hiring manager and department. Identifying poor line managers who consistently turnover staff versus their peers can help the company save significant resources by identifying action plans such as training or other management interventions. By analyzing this data, you may also help the business define which areas will consistently have higher than average turnover rates and be able to manage to those constraints.

Managing Down. HR generally understands the specific metrics here, using termination surveys examining top reasons for leaving, compensation questions, management questions, and so on. One of the easiest mistakes to make in separation data is to show executives separation data they don't particularly care about. Which statistics are more actionable to an executive manager? The 90/120 turnover rate before and after implementing a validated assessment with cost savings? Or the voluntary turnover rate by department?

CHAPTER

7

Missions, Objectives, and Metrics

Correlating Performance and Goals

A company without a mission is like a ship without a compass; whether the captain turns left or right, he must know in which direction his craft is sailing. Even with the sail (technology) in place and the sailors working diligently, without a mapped course the ship will not swiftly reach any desired destination.

Likewise, without a destination in mind, a company can be easily blown off-course by customer budget and staffing concerns. The fundamentals of performance are missions and objectives. Having departmental missions and objectives that correlate with the company-wide mission helps assure that the practices remain focused.

Similarly, the performance of the individual correlates with the performance of the entire organization, just as acquiring a baseball player with high stats will not improve the team's record if the rest of the players are not training or reaching their potential. A team must be able to work closely together to accomplish their goals.

It's not just the top performers that are essential for company-wide

71

success. For example, Barry Bonds is arguably one of the greatest home run hitters of all time, but the San Francisco Giants are not a perennial powerhouse like the Yankees. Individual employees need to have clear work objectives, which are based on their departmental and company-wide mission. The metrics by which they are measured should both fit into their individual performance measures and directly relate to the broader corporate objectives.

It is also important to consider performance measurement within the context of a firm's mission. Malcolm Gladwell highlights this idea in his recent *New Yorker* article entitled "Game Theory," where he describes the book *The Wages of Wins* by economists David J. Berri, Martin B. Schmidt, and Stacey L. Brook.

According to their work, most of the statistics used to evaluate a player's effectiveness are not relevant to the team's overall mission: winning. "The economists have developed a metric or 'algorithm' that they call a Win Score, because it expresses a player's worth compared to the number of wins his contributions bring to his team." (Gladwell 2006) It is important in the development of any metric that performance is not measured relative only to peers or some other generic benchmark, but rather incorporates the objectives and overall mission of the department and organization.

Developing a framework for assessing the connection between individual performance and corporate success is the charge of the Human Resources department as a whole. Identifying and measuring the cost of human capital and its relationship to corporate performance can be done through a variety of processes. In most cases it behooves Human Resources to focus first on their mission, develop specific objectives, identify a clear strategy to accomplish the objectives, and then measure their performance with metrics. The evaluation process is cyclical, since each step should follow from the last and metrics are then used to evaluate the overall mission, objectives, and strategy.

Establishing the mission for staffing and human capital management is as critical as establishing the mission for the organization as a whole. The mission objectives will quickly materialize and strategy often seems initially clear, but getting it right takes detailed, consistent and regular measurement.

Applying metrics to staffing and human capital measurement is the key to avoiding complaisance and getting the process right. A process that is as involved and subtle as measuring human capital requires a great deal of rigor and should incorporate much more than broad generalizations.

Assessing the performance of individuals requires more than a rough, entirely qualitative understanding of how their performance affects overall corporate performance. Just as early sailing vessels relied on astronomy and the astrolabe to chart their uncertain courses, qualitative staffing assessments help identify obvious areas for improvement in staffing, but they will almost certainly omit the finer details necessary to specific, actionable improvements in staffing objectives and strategy. Developing metrics that assess staffing objectives and strategy will help companies chart a more precise and accurate course.

Some factors to keep in mind when measuring individual performance are goals, self-awareness, empathy and relationships, capacity, external factors, organizational compatibility, influencer impact, compensation and other requirements, motivation, aspirations, and potential.

Often, technology affects the performance and function of the individual. For example, it used to take several pilots and co-pilots to operate a passenger plane. With the current on–board computers and radar systems, a passenger plane generally requires only one pilot and one co-pilot to operate.

Staffing metrics may be likened to John Harrison's nautical chronometer that provided superior sailing navigation accuracy in the eighteenth century as compared to the astronomical approaches that were used up to that time. However, as Dava Sobel explains in her book, *Longitude: The True Story of a Lone Genius Who Solved the Greatest Scientific Problem of His Time*, Harrison struggled for many years to win widespread acceptance for his chronometer.

Staffing metrics are also gaining increased popularity as professionals seek to improve their processes, but they are still underutilized by many firms. However, the increased accuracy and precision of staffing analysis through metrics may place these quantitative measures in the records of staffing history just as the triumph of the chronometer placed it in the records of maritime history.

Because implemented metrics that are well-designed help bridge the divide between the corporate mission and individual performance, they should be used in assessing the employees, or what is termed the human capital cycle, within staffing operations. The human capital cycle is an essential process within staffing and serves as the framework for developing, deploying, and improving the human capital of the firm. We can define the closed loop human capital cycle as acquisition, performance (including performance indicators and performance results) assessment, development, retention, and change of human capital within the organization. The cycle of human capital corresponds to staffing effectiveness and has the power to increase or diminish corporate profitability.

Human capital within the organization may be divided into several categories such as part-time and full-time employees, exempt and nonexempt employees, interns, consultants, and contractors. No matter how the human capital is divided, the closed loop cycle and the way in which it is acquired, assessed, performed, developed, retained, and changed depends heavily on the mission and objectives of staffing operations. Within this context, appropriate metrics should be developed for each company to analyze the entire human capital cycle.

The performance of human capital is the most obvious application for performance metrics, but should be divided into performance indicators and organizational results. Metrics should also be readily applied to human capital assessment, such as the readiness, depth, turnover vulnerability, diversity, and succession planning of an organization's human capital. However, straightforward metrics may also be applied to the acquisition, development, retention, and change management of human capital.

Working with Metrics to Evaluate Human Capital

CLOSED LOOP HUMAN CAPITAL CYCLE

- Acquisition.
- Performance.
  - Key performance indicators.
  - Organization results.
- Assessment.
  - Readiness, depth, vulnerability, diversity, succession planning.
- Development.
- Retention.
- Change.

Since staffing metrics are not pervasive in all of staffing management, it is sometimes challenging to implement quantitative measures into staffing operations. Adopting a five-step process with those who carry out the staffing mission may help to implement staffing metrics.

The first step is to stress the value of metrics in the development of an *individual's* career, which may help to garner support. Secondly, emphasizing metrics across all Human Resources staff departments can help create the "we're all in this together mentality." Third, make the metrics relevant to staffing processes with clear links to improvements that may benefit the Human Resources department as a whole.

Fourth, a gradual stepped implementation of one or two metrics at a time will help change perceptions of the metrics. And finally, let staff members track their own performance through metrics before reporting publicly or using them as formal evaluation tools. Once implemented, managers should work to build a culture around the metrics to further their integration and encourage utilization on an individual level. Stress the value of metrics to their careers both within the company and beyond.

AFTER IMPLEMENTATION

1. Host routine monthly performance metrics reviews.
2. Recognize superior performance, such as best and most improved in every possible category.
3. Encourage sharing—informal coaching.
4. Experiment—don't be afraid of adverse results. They are necessary to achieve the highest levels of performance.
5. Pay close attention to activity indicators to preclude bad results.

EXECUTIVE REPORTING

1. Don't look back—start with current data.
2. Don't overwhelm people with data—a single, simple-to-read page is best.
3. Once you start reporting, make sure you don't stop—keep it on time, every time.
4. Answer questions before they're asked; if the data raises a question, answer it with the report.

Let people draw their own conclusions.

The development of Human Resources metrics relates to the direct correlation between individual performance and the company's performance as a whole. However, the degree and number of employees varies. If you find it difficult to measure human capital, defined by Margaret M. Blair, co-author of the Brookings Institution study, "Understanding Intangible Sources of Value," as "part of a set of intangibles that a company simply cannot control: the way employees work together, not just the sum of what an individual knows" (Workforce Management 2001) blueprinting may be the solution you are looking for. Undoubtedly, Human Resources professionals throughout the past several decades experienced frustration when trying to measure human capital. Then, as now, leaders are always looking for the solution to issues that arise as a result of differing personalities.

As is often the case today, this solution addressed one aspect of human capital. After force was no longer effective or permissible, managers often responded by replacing people. Now many also tend to focus on a single solution such as a selection program or management practice. Most improvements provide some benefit, but inevitably problems reappear in one form or another.

While fixing problems as they occur may seem to save long hours of evaluating and planning, a more proactive approach is the most effective one. Individuals are too complex and teams and organizations are correspondingly more so. For example, in the mid-seventies, a U.S. government task force researched selection, training, and management for special operations units. One of the outcomes that they discovered was a multifaceted template that connected elements of the work, the operating unit, and individuals. The task force recognized not just the connectivity and complexity of human performance but also that a holistic approach offered the best basis for making decisions about people.

Measuring intangible human capital has caused countless headaches for Human Resources professionals throughout the years. According to Workforce Management, experts in the field are beginning to "ask the right questions," evaluating, according to Blair, "how to value the productivity and future benefit additions to human capital: the skills, talents and capabilities that are really embedded in people." (Workforce Management 2001) Again, it all goes back to the mission and objectives. Staffing expert Nick Burkholder recommends the five following steps toward creating an effective framework for measuring human capital. The more clarity is around the first two steps, the easier the strategy will be to identify. And the more aligned the objectives are with the organizational mission, the more beneficial the strategy will be to the organization.

1. Determine the mission.
2. Identify specific goals and objectives.
3. Develop the strategy to attain those goals and objectives.
4. Design the process, organization, and structure to execute the strategy.
5. Measure and report.

Every department mission should support the mission of the organization.

- There can be no HR mission without an organization mission.
- Generals are responsible for establishing military objectives—not colonels, not majors, not captains, and certainly not lieutenants.
- The objectives are important and they require time and effort.
- The ability to establish the right objectives is the most important leadership responsibility.

Organization's mission questions:

- Does it make sense?
  - Management.
  - Employees.
  - Customers.
- Will it still be valid?
  - Tomorrow.
  - In a month.
  - In a year.

HR mission questions:

- Does it completely support the organization's mission?
- Does it make sense? Does it say the same thing to management, employees, and even external constituencies?
- Will it stand the test of time?

The Human Capital Blueprint™

When evaluating the individual human capital performance, it's often difficult to maintain consistent input data that remains uniform throughout the information gathering process. For example, if you have a group of 20 mountaineers who set out to climb Mount Everest, there are several objectives to meet in order to accomplish that mission. One of the first and most important steps is to ensure that the climbers have supplies before they embark on their climb. The supply objective is critical to meeting other objectives that will lead to the completion of the goal, which is reaching the summit of Mount Everest.

This obviously takes some coordination, and meeting this objective requires significant discussion among all 20 climbers. If that's the case, then the outcome is that they will have 100 percent of the supplies they need when they reach the base of the mountain. However, there may have been unforeseen circumstances or a communication breakdown, perhaps forgetting some supplies or someone missing the rendezvous point, which will result in a less than perfect outcome.

Climbing Mount Everest is a very expensive endeavor, so let's assume that the mountaineers are well-funded and purchase the additional necessary supplies at the bottom of the mountain, assuming they are available. The outcome would be that they garnered all necessary supplies, but did so at a greater expense than if they had been able to craft a perfect packing list, communicate it flawlessly to everyone, and have all 20 climbers pack without error. The degree to which the climbers fell short could easily be measured by the additional markup paid to buy their supplies at the base of the mountain.

At this point the climbers have met their objective, albeit at a higher cost than if they had executed flawlessly, and they may now progress to the next objective of climbing to summit. In their mission to climb Mount Everest, they have now accomplished one objective of gathering all necessary supplies and preparing to embark on the climb. No doubt this is only one of a host of objectives necessary to climb the mountain, but the outcome of meeting this objective is the opportunity to climb to the base camp, which moves them one step closer to reaching the summit. The imperfection of their execution meant that they spent more time than they would have otherwise.

Climbing Mount Everest is usually a once-in-a-lifetime experience, but let's say that this group of 20 mountaineers is commissioned by the Nepalese government to conduct scientific experiments over the course of several expeditions. In this case, the cost of the climb is important, since the climb will be repeated sev-

eral times. It is critical to measure the level of success of each outcome and the number of objectives met. Since we are now assuming that the climbers need to repeat their ascent several times, it is
important to measure the degree to which each objective was satisfied, since each objective is essential to making the mission successful. Let's consider only one objective: ensuring that they
brought all the necessary supplies. To measure the climbers' effectiveness, we first need to separate the flaws in the objective (did
the climbers properly consider all the supplies they would need?)
versus the flaws in the communication and execution necessary for
the climbers to meet the objectives.

Since we assume the climbers are to undertake this expedition several times, it is important to measure the degree to which they met
the objective, where the error occurred, and the magnitude of the error. The metrics the climbers use to evaluate their progress are based
on their objectives developed within the context of the mission.

The Human Capital Blueprint™ is based on three dimensions of
human capital. It was created to provide comprehensive guidelines
based on metrics and expert experience and opinion. Focusing on
the factors, staffing, and the cycle of human capital helps to break
the blueprinting task into manageable sections, each with its own
mission, objectives, and metrics under the larger company mission.
The most revealing part of the Blueprint is the "blueprinting"
process itself. Just by working through the process, your view of the
organization changes and you can start adjustments almost immediately. Though linked, each dimension has distinct human capital
management applications.

Factors. First, the factors that drive organizational and individual
performance enable you to design or evaluate an organization; create a position description; evaluate a candidate or employee. There
are fundamental and operational factors. Fundamental organizational factors include mission and leadership and are the basis of
any enterprise. Operational factors relate to executing and delivering and include objectives, strategy, and design and structure.

Staffing. The second dimension, staffing, addresses the different types of human capital. This includes every category of employee as well as contractors, consultants, temps, and even outsourced operations. Today, no matter what type of employee, from a contractor to full-time or outsource, the category of human capital has become incidental. Evaluating and planning enables companies to compare the different categories and classifications of human capital necessary for any level of work. The categories include part-time and full-time employees, and the types of human capital include employees, contractors, and completely outsourced operations.

Cycle. Third, the cycle includes the acquisition, development, and retention of all types and categories of human capital, as well as the ultimate measure of human capital: organizational and individual performance.

WHEN MEASURING HUMAN CAPITAL

1. *Keep track of data.* It is important to have the necessary data available. For example, it is impossible to calculate cost ratio and efficiency without first knowing your organization's external and internal recruiting expenses.

2. *Measure consistently.* Be careful not to overdo it; calculating quality, time, satisfaction, RCR, and efficiency more than once a month can distort the results.

3. *Monitor activity indicators weekly.* Activity indicators, such as Acceptance-to-Start Ratio, should be monitored every week. The trends that these results yield, both positive and negative, should be examined closely.

4. *Make adjustments.* Be sure to correct the negative trends, while exploiting the positive ones.

5. *Don't be afraid to experiment,* even if it may or does produce negative results. No performance curves go straight up; Look for mistakes. Things are never as bad, or good, as they seem.

The five main components of the blueprinting process include gathering information, analyzing information, validating the analyses, envisioning what can be, and creating an action plan to achieve the blueprinting goals.

Gather Information. The blueprinting process begins as information related to the three human capital dimensions is collected.

Analyze the Information. The collected data alone will provide helpful evaluative data for existing organizations. The lack of clear or correct mission and objectives, for example, is a common cause of poor performance. Startups can use the analyses to determine the optimum human capital allocations and categories.

Validate the Analyses. It is critical that all appropriate constituencies validate the analyses. Fundamental organizational factors are particularly critical, for they are the major drivers for all human capital performance.

Envision. Envisioning enables what can be to become a reality.

Blueprint for Action. Blueprinting ends with a documented plan and the associated metrics that will deliver the optimum human capital and organizational performance.

While each dimension is clearly separate, they all influence the others. Whether applied to employees, contractors, or temps, the factors that drive the performance of every type of human capital have a similar life cycle. The activities may be different for employees and outsourced operations, but the life cycle should be the same. A metric or benchmark is much more meaningful if you have associated information on the other types of human capital and the other dimensions.

Measuring Individual Human Capital Performance

Modeling its system after one developed by Jack Welch, former CEO of General Electric, Goodyear graded all salaried employees on a curve; the bottom 10 percent were denied bonuses and raises and told that they might lose their jobs. Some did.

Goodyear ended its two-year-old system just as a class-action discrimination lawsuit was filed against the company. And Goodyear isn't the only company that had to face issues arising from implementing these rankings: Ford, Capital One, Conoco, and Microsoft have all learned that designing and implementing an effective forced ranking system is a formidable and often legal challenge.

POINTERS

- The evaluation should foster desired performance as well as accurately measure job performance.
- The evaluation should be integrated fully within the organization's entire human capital management system.
- Forced ranking systems invariably add an internal competition dynamic to an organizational culture. Competition and individual performance are highest when a group of individuals knows that they will all be ranked.
- As human capital metrics become more prevalent, it will be easier to compare current and prospective employees. Then organizations will compete to recruit the best performers in any field.

WARNINGS

- It is inappropriate and ineffective to use ratings to drive a decrease in the workforce or to compensate for organizational flaws such as a lack of leadership.
- On its own, an employee performance rating system cannot change an organization's culture or ultimate performance.

- Introducing forced rankings to an established culture is very difficult and can actually undermine performance for some time. Eventually, those employees who do not embrace the competitive dynamics either leave of their own accord or get the lowest ranking and are dismissed.

When establishing metrics for individual measures, some factors to consider are production, efficiency and time, satisfaction, quality, and time to measure. When discussing new hire quality, it is not about the specific new hires, it's about whether they meet the hiring objectives and about the hiring program itself and the development that is applied to the new hire. You can evaluate the new hire performance in light of the initial recruiting objectives. To help evaluate the development program, measure different new hires at different points. This tells you where the weaknesses are in each area.

For example, if you are measuring the position of file clerk, the time to measure would be between four to six weeks. Other factors to consider include measuring customer feedback and the number of files per hour with a quality benchmark of 99 percent accuracy. If evaluating a staffing director, the goal might be plus or minus 5 percent of national benchmarks with 85 percent satisfaction and 90 percent quality hires over a period of nine months. Table 7.1 shows examples of new hire quality definitions and when they should be measured.

Measuring individual contributors. An individual contributor's mission should be the main purpose for which the individual is employed or contracted. Ask these questions as you draft the mission:

- Does it completely support the group or organization mission?
- Does it make sense and mean the same thing to all participants including management, internal or external customers, and other associates?
- Will it stand the test of time?

Table 7.1

Position	Quality Defined			Time to Measure
	Production, Efficiency, and Time	Satisfaction	Quality	
File Clerk	100 files per hour	Associate/ Customer Feedback	99% Accuracy	Four to Six Weeks
Analyst	Number of Cases per day	Associate/ Customer Feedback	90% Accuracy	Three Months
Vice President, Global Sales	Gross and Net Revenues	Customer Feedback	Retention	One Year
Staffing Director	+/−5% National Benchmarks	85% Satisfied or Better	90% Quality Hires	Nine Months

An individual recruiter's mission might be: "To be a highly-rated field sales recruiter through a process of hiring manager driven continuous improvement."

Establish objectives. Individual contributor objectives should be specific and measurable deliverables that are essential to fulfilling the mission. The best objectives are jointly established with customers. Keep these points in mind as you develop them:

- Do they support every aspect of the mission?
- Do they leave anything out?
- Are they measurable?
- Are they clear to all constituencies including management, internal or external customers, and other associates?
- Double check to hear what the customers think of them.
- Associate metrics with each objective.

Organizational Missions, Objectives and Metrics

Whether you are an HR metrics veteran or are just beginning to implement individual and company-wide performance initiatives, the most important thing to keep in mind is first, creating mission and objectives and second, building your measurement strategy on the framework laid out by the mission and objectives.

The broader scope of company-wide mission and objectives serves to unify employees in different departments as they work toward a similar goal under the umbrella of the corporate mission. With a mission to meet, objectives begin to become apparent and can then be broken down into departmental objectives as individual employees work together to accomplish the mission.

For example, if the mountain climbers' mission includes hang-gliding back down the mountain once they reach the half-way marker, they need to check their maps against the terrain, dig up rocks to avoid crashing, and possibly create a makeshift runway to land on, all before they begin their climb to the summit. The climbers need to work together as one cohesive unit, each one thoroughly examining their designated section of terrain to see if it correlates with the mapped route and make corrections or find alternate routes where necessary.

While the mission is essential, one without specific, measurable objectives is simply empty words on paper. If the climbers did not determine their objectives, how do they get to each marker along the way and complete the tasks necessary to reach those markers? Most likely, they end up wasting valuable resources determining their course of action on the spot. Revisiting the mission and objectives as a routine part of regular meetings helps to ensure resiliency and interdepartmental communication. In another example, although a ship's captain may have a destination in mind, he also needs to know how to route the ship around brewing storms while still making time. Without following the ship's log to help check off daily maintenance tasks he would waste valuable time and resources.

SAMPLE OBJECTIVES

Quality people in all positions recognizing the great value in diversity. Acquiring the most qualified applicants for each department while appreciating the different skill sets, backgrounds, and perspectives that each employee brings to the table. Having qualified employees who recognize the advantages of diversity and can work as a unified team enables employees to draw upon one another's strengths and solidify their skill sets to benefit the organization. Based on a 0–5 point scale, one example may include an average new hire quality rating of 3.75 based on prerecruiting requirements and an average employee performance rating of 3.5 based on position performance standards. Objectives may include completing an organization audit annually, establishing succession and development plans for all critical employees, and establishing and following development plans for 70 percent of all employees.

Highly rated HR performance. One of the great untapped roles of HR is to help the organization and subordinate units establish the mission and objectives. Human capital is essential to most, if not every, company function. Human Resources works to acquire, develop, and retain the human capital at the heart of business operations.

Competitive efficiency. Providing comfortable working conditions, attractive benefits such as a 401K with employer match and/or tuition reimbursement helps organizations remain competitively efficient compared to others of the same industry and size. Maintaining their recruiting cost ratio is also a marker of competitive efficiency. For example, sample objectives may include working to ensure that compensation for 75 percent of job groups is within 5 percent of associated benchmarks and that all HR costs are within 5 percent of associated benchmarks.

Why measure? Metrics help organizations to understand and identify whether human capital is meeting corporate objectives. Using the climber example, if they didn't keep track of how much money they spent they wouldn't understand how important to their overall budget it is that they pack enough supplies and not rely on more expensive supply stations. Whether working to create and evaluate value for acquisition, performance, assessment, development, retention, or change management areas of human capital management, it is important to understand how company resources are being allocated.

How to measure. The reason for working to implement a framework to measure human capital is to meet objectives based on the company mission. No matter which measures you choose, they are effective only if linked to company missions and objectives. Pete Ramstead, executive vice president of strategy and finance for Personnel Decisions International in Minneapolis, says "For example, [with] cost-to-hire and time-to-fill, without any way to measure how good the candidates are that you're hiring, you understand only efficiency, not effectiveness."

In 1997 Ramstead and John Boudreau, director of Cornell University's Center for Advanced HR studies, created the Human Capital Bridge Framework, "which enables companies to translate what employees do into financial capital." Ramstead and Boudreau suggest asking the following seven questions before designing or implementing a measurement system:

1. Are the connections between the human capital metrics and the ultimate successes of the organization clear and compelling?

2. When the organization's strategies change, do the measures identify where human capital strategies need to change?

3. Does the measurement system support the development of human capital strategies tailored to the organization's unique competitive advantage?

4. Will the measurement system drive distinctive human capital investments to the talent group that has the potential to have the greatest economic effect?

5. Can the measurement system support decisions about HR programs before they are implemented?

6. Can the measurement system reveal when HR programs should be discontinued?

7. Does the measurement framework identify how talent creates value within the organization in a way that is understandable and motivating to all employees?

What to Measure? Determining which measures apply to your company can be challenging to say the least. Once you have a blueprint, choosing the types of measurement methods is much simpler. However, each department and situation warrants a different approach. Using the measures of new hire quality, hiring manager satisfaction, and others creates a base to build upon when working to establish a system to measure human capital.

Noted academic Richard Swanson from the University of Minnesota delivered a keynote session at the 2003 Human Capital Metrics Summit, titled "Ensuring Valuable Outcomes from Human Resource Investments." Dr. Swanson's presentation addressed the HR Performance Challenge, Thinking Tools, and a Fast Track to Assessing Performance. His Performance Diagnosis Matrix is a classic and invaluable to effectively understanding any organization.

HR Metrics Defined—Performance Diagnosed

PERFORMANCE DIAGNOSIS MATRIX OF ENABLING QUESTIONS

Table 7.2 shows Dr. Swanson's Performance Diagnosis Matrix.

Table 7.2

Performance Variables	Performance Levels		
	Organization Level	Process Level	Individual Level
Mission/Goal	Does the organization mission/goal fit the reality of the economic, political, and cultural forces?	Do the process goals enable the organization to meet the organization and individual mission/goals?	Are the professional and personal mission/goals of individuals congruent with the organization?
System Design	Does the organization system provide structure and policies supporting the desired performance?	Are processes designed in such a way to work as a system?	Does the individual face obstacles that impede job performance?
Capacity	Does the organization have the leadership, capital, and infrastructure to achieve its mission/goals?	Does the process have the capacity to perform (quantity, quality and timeliness)?	Does the individual have the mental, physical, and emotional capacity to perform?
Motivation	Do the policies, culture, and reward systems support the desired performance?	Does the process provide the information and human factors required to maintain it?	Does the individual want to perform no matter what?
Expertise	Does the organization establish and maintain selection and training policies and resources?	Does the process of developing expertise meet the changing demands of changing processes?	Does the individual have the knowledge, skills, and experience to perform?

91

Swanson's four Principles of Practice are also very helpful when establishing metrics:

1. Start with defining the primary performance outputs of the organization.
2. Identify the core organization process(es).
3. Position HR as a major organization process designed to maintain or improve core organization process performance.
4. Work with a well-defined performance improvement process, work with internal partners, and call upon an eclectic set of interventions.

When striving to integrate and meet individual, departmental, and company-wide human capital benchmarks, according to Ramstead, "Value is determined by measuring which talent pools are critical to a company's success." Having specific criteria for measuring core organizational processes and essential positions along with an eye for customer care and a focus on retention strategy helps to minimize hiring mistakes, create a more streamlined process and a more organized, positive, working environment.

Because it's virtually impossible to measure strategy or practices, focusing on performance metrics that have measurable results yields more effective, more accurate data with which to evaluate human capital. Metrics used to measure human capital should be developed within the context of the mission and objectives laid out for the individuals being measured and are always considered in that context. This also permits more accurate analysis of the correlation between individual performance and overall corporate performance. When all crew members, from the deck hands to the captain, are regularly checking off their lists to meet objectives related to achieving the mission, the ship is better able to avoid obstacles, conserve resources, and ride out inevitable storms.

Measuring Staffing—A Better Approach to Hiring Metrics

As human capital management continues to be a major business imperative, providing a framework for making good decisions regarding such human assets is becoming essential. As mentioned in Chapter 3, underlying human capital decision science are the methodologies, systems, and tools, including the metrics that support the decision making process as it relates to human capital and the impact to the organization. However, a decision framework for understanding the human component of an organization's asset base is still relatively new and has only recently received significant attention.

Most decisions regarding the investments a company makes to acquire, deploy, develop, or retain its human capital are still primarily based on internal Human Resources efficiency metrics and are of limited value in supporting human capital decision making by the rest of the organization. Efficiency-type measures typically gauge the performance of Human Resources functions or processes, such as staffing, and although important, are generally not tightly aligned with the mission of the organization. They focus on identifying the level of human resource programs generated for a given investment of resources—like time and money—and tend to be numbers driven. Typical examples of these staffing metrics include vacancy/fill rates, internal cycle times, and cost-per-hire or other cost elements. These measures help identify issues that need correcting by measuring the performance of Human Resources programs or processes.

As noted in the earlier chapters, many leaders are now arguing that the measurement of employee performance should be the primary focus of metrics since human capital (the employees), is the most critical asset to achieving an organization's mission. They emphasize that measuring Human Resources processes and programs is important, but maintain that employee performance-focused metrics linked to business strategy should be of paramount concern. Unlike efficiency-type measures, these metrics are typically more subjective and enterprise-wide, helping to support human capital decision making across the organization. They focus on directly measuring employee performance and the effectiveness of related programs and processes and can be employed throughout the different phases of the employee lifecycle. Examples of these metrics can include quality of new hires, customer (hiring manager or employee) satisfaction, productivity, and internal mobility measures, as well as retention measures of high performance employees. This chapter will examine the key metrics available during the attraction and acquisition or staffing phase of the employee lifecycle and discuss their application in organizations today.

Although organizations have been using metrics since Xerox first popularized performance measurement as part of the benchmarking movement more than 20 years ago, it was Staffing.org that first provided a set of standard metrics to measure the performance of staffing operations that is still used today. Since the late 1990s, Staffing.org has been conducting an annual Recruiting Metrics & Benchmark Survey and publishing a benchmark report on the performance of staffing operations across a range of industries. Offering a superior alternative to the limitations of traditional staffing metrics, the report provides organizations four proven performance metrics, including both efficiency and effectiveness measures, to utilize in evaluating their staffing efforts and in measuring the performance of new employees. The 2006 Recruiting Metrics and Performance Benchmark Report captures financial data from more than 4,000 organizations and examines performance data related to New Hire Quality, Hiring Manager Satisfaction, Time, Cost, Efficiency, and more. Each of the five metrics will be discussed.

New Hire Quality

It can be argued that of the metrics discussed, New Hire Quality is one of the most important. A recent survey conducted by HRMetrics.org found that more than 19,000 C-level executives rated new hire quality as having the highest level of importance when compared with 20-plus other HR metrics (9.6 on a ten point scale). As little as seven years ago, according to the latest Staffing.org Benchmark Report, more than 90 percent of organizations in the United States insisted that New Hire Quality was critical, yet less than 2 percent of them were making any attempt to measure it. In that same Staffing.org report, respondents were asked to prioritize their metrics foci for next year—over 58 percent selected quality, more than any other choice. Today, over 40 percent of organizations have some sort of New Hire Quality measurement.

Despite agreement by both CFOs and chief HR officers that people and talent are crucial, it's somewhat surprising that organizations have been slow to measure the quality of their new employees.

One possible reason for this is that the New Hire Quality metric cannot be defined by a specific formula. Instead, it is defined by staffing and business stakeholders working together. The standards for New Hire Quality should be determined by the hiring manager before recruiting is initiated, and the quality measure should be taken within the first 90 to 180 days of employment (depending on the predetermined requirements set by the hiring manager). This is after the easiest and hardest periods of new hire assimilation and also, before the organizational influences significantly impact the rating. In short, New Hire Quality is:

- Performance criteria established by the hiring manager prior to initiating recruitment.
- New hire performance associated with recruiting standards.
- Measured at a predetermined point in time.

Since the process for assessing quality of staffing operations cannot be based on a specific formula, gathering additional information is beneficial. If hiring managers track the data above, they will be able to determine:

- Whether operations align with the business as evidenced by the success of new hires once they have started.
- Whether you are producing highly rated hires that are truly prepared to have the impact on the business that they are expected to have. (Are you hiring people who have the qualifications necessary to be successful in your system, or are you simply matching resume entries with job specifications?)

Time

Recruiting time questions have ranked in the top three inquiries received by Staffing.org since becoming an independent corporation in 1998. Proper implementation of time improves the relationship between hiring manager and recruiter, making for a more effective hiring process and yielding better results.

More than 10 years ago, when the phrase just-in-time recruiting became popular, many thought it marked the beginning of a new stage in the profession. We were going to advance recruiting as the manufacturing profession had recently advanced it. And most importantly, the fruit of our labor was going to be respected. Just-in-time recruiting certainly resonates with hiring managers, but we didn't take the time to understand how just-in-time works in the manufacturing industry.

Just-in-time is a sound inventory and manufacturing management practice. It wasn't started so much to speed up delivery or manufacturing but rather to minimize capital tied up in inventory and storage. The associated financial benefits are significant. And it works. The organizations that are responsible for delivering just-in-time use detailed and sophisticated timelines to understand all components of the process and give the customer what they want, when they want it. It doesn't matter how long it takes for the steel, or silicon chips, or chemicals, or tires, or whatever, to be delivered. All that matters is that they are delivered when they are needed and expected based on the terms jointly contracted by the manufacturer and supplier.

Time-to-Fill and Time-to-Start are popular traditional human resource metrics, utilizing time rather than number of hires as a measure of staffing efficiency. These measures are subject to several limitations and weaknesses. Both measures are easy to manipulate and are at the mercy of unforeseen business or personal demands beyond the control or purview of staffing operations. You can ask staffing professionals and they can easily recall experiences filling positions in what they believe to be a timely manner only to be told by an unhappy hiring manager that they needed someone "yesterday." Time metrics that don't specify an agreed-upon criteria and timeframe are by definition doomed to fail right from the start since no mutual understanding has been established.

Actual and Contracted Time-to-Start addresses this issue. Prior to beginning the recruiting process for a new position, the hiring manager and recruiter should negotiate a Time-to-Start for the position. This ensures more realistic expectations of when someone will start working. This becomes the Contracted Time-to-Start. The Actual Time-to-Start is the average number of days between the first day of recruiting for a position and the first day new employees are on the job. Note the difference from Time-to-Acceptance, which focuses on number of days to fill the position. The Time-to-Start is a more important number, since most hiring managers care more about when a person will start working. Prior to beginning the recruiting process for a new position, the hiring manager and recruiter should negotiate a Time-to-Start for the position. This ensures more realistic expectations of when someone will start working. This becomes the Contracted Time-to-Start.

The Time metric encourages recruiters to meet with hiring managers and discuss these issues and the joint responsibility involved in filling the position in question. Sample timelines, including roles and responsibilities, are especially helpful to accurate contracting. The outcome of this discussion is a negotiated, realistic target start date. The hiring manager and recruiter should be working together to achieve this goal. As with the best metrics, this one fosters high performance by:

- Creating shared ownership of the process with hiring managers.
- Encouraging hiring managers to include recruiting in their human capital planning.
- Allowing recruiters to jointly establish realistic expectations with hiring managers.

- Allowing recruiters to focus on quality as well as Time-to-Start.

The Actual Time-to-Start is divided by the Contracted Time-to-Start and then multiplied by 100 to yield a percentage. Outcomes of 100 percent or less indicate that new employees are starting on or before the contracted time, while percentages over 100 indicate that recruiting efforts are taking longer than expected.

$$\text{Time} = \frac{\text{Actual Time-to-Start}}{\text{Contracted Time-to-Start}}$$

The value of using a ratio instead of a difference (that is, Actual Time-to-Start minus Contracted Time-to-Start) is that the ratio better accounts for the initial hiring manager expectations and needs in contracting. Consider ratios for two positions that each are filled 14 days later than promised. The first has been contracted for four weeks (28 days) but actually takes six weeks to fill (42 days). The ratio calculation is $42/28 \times 100 = 150\%$, or 50 percent longer than promised. The second position has been contracted for 12 weeks (84 days) and takes fourteen weeks (98 days) to fill. This ratio calculation is $98/84 \times 100 = 116\%$, or about 16 percent longer than promised. The higher ratio in the first instance captures the fact that a two-week delay is more problematic when a hiring manager has contracted to fill a position quickly. The straight difference between Actual and Contracted Time-to-Start (14 days for both positions) misses this important point.

The Time metric recognizes that filling the position is a joint responsibility between recruitment and the hiring department and encourages both parties to negotiate a realistic contracted date that can be changed upon mutual consent and prevailing business conditions. This level of partnership provides a constructive way to deal with changing priorities and other issues that inevitably occur and adversely impact the hiring process.

Although this metric is expressed as a ratio, actual time measures to fill specific positions can be used as sample timelines and can be helpful when planning to fill similar positions in future efforts. As mentioned earlier, this metric helps create a shared ownership of the hiring process, a key advantage over traditional time metrics and reflective of current business practices, which stress having management involvement in talent acquisition. It helps to address the "communication gap" that is frequently cited in business literature as existing between Human Resources (HR) and hiring management. Hiring managers directly participating in a collaborative recruiting system are more likely to have their needs and issues addressed because they can actively own their part of the recruiting process while communicating effectively with other participants.

Hiring Manager Satisfaction

Also known as Customer Satisfaction, this is the hiring manager's satisfaction rating for the hiring process. Hiring Manager Satisfaction has been traditionally measured after the recruiting process has been completed. However, there is an inherent problem with this approach: namely, the hiring manager has no preestablished guidelines by which to judge the recruiter. A better questionnaire is one that is completed before and after the recruitment process of a new position. This ensures that everyone is clear about expectations.

It is common in industry today for companies to measure the satisfaction of customers with the products or services they have purchased. Many of these efforts provide insightful information and help guide product and service level improvements. However, efforts to measure the satisfaction of hiring managers (as customers) with their staffing services have generally proved to be of limited value. Typically assessed after the fact, if at all, and on an ad-hoc individual manager basis, many of these approaches have provided one-sided information offering little about improving staffing effectiveness to help achieve business goals. The inherent problem with this approach is that the hiring manager has no preestablished guidelines by which to judge the recruiter. A better technique is a questionnaire that is completed before and after the recruitment process of a new position. This ensures that everyone is clear about expectations. Measuring Hiring Manager Satisfaction only after the cycle is completed invalidates the entire process.

Often achieving hiring manager satisfaction in one particular part of the organization occurs by dedicating already limited staffing resources at the expense of other parts of the organization. To that end, staffing professionals operating without agreed upon staffing criteria will never be able to satisfy all hiring managers since their expectations will vary based on their past experiences, both positive and negative. Staffing.org's approach and accompanying tool to measure hiring manager satisfaction provides a proven method to clarify hiring manager expectations on the front end and then to evaluate performance against such expectations after the hire. Clarifying and understanding the hiring manager's needs and expectations before the start of the search provides the staffing professional with an opportunity to begin with "the end in mind" and avoid the fundamental flaw of most customer satisfaction measures—not knowing what is important to the customer.

Staffing.org's Staffing Metrics Toolkit provides a customer satisfaction survey template that has been field-tested and is relatively easy to customize. The template uses a five-point rating scale and lists a variety of rating criteria by which to rate the recruiter and the staffing experience, such as understanding of the position, understanding of the market, sourcing options, assessment of candidates, communications, offer/closing effectiveness, timeliness, quality and quantity of candidates, and so on. The template also helps the staffing professional to facilitate a discussion of the manager's expectations and requirements. When the hiring manager is asked to complete the survey shortly after the hire, he/she will recognize that the evaluation factors used are the same ones that the staffing professional discussed to clarify expectations before recruiting was initiated. An average hiring manager rating is then easily calculated and can serve as a sound measure of recruiting effectiveness.

However, Staffing.org's own research suggests that measuring hiring manager satisfaction, at least formally, is not typically done on a regular basis in most organizations. This is a lost opportunity for organizations, as preliminary research indicates that organizations that regularly measure hiring manager satisfaction report higher levels of satisfaction by hiring managers with their recruiting process as compared to organizations that only occasionally measure manager satisfaction (Recruiting Metrics & Performance Benchmark Report, 2005). Although research in this area is still relatively limited, it stands to reason that engaging in measurement on a regular basis will require increased collaboration between Human Resources and hiring managers, which in turn is likely to improve the staffing process as observed by improved hiring manager satisfaction ratings.

Such has been the case for the Coors Brewing Company in research conducted by the Corporate Executive Board's Recruiting Roundtable. Coors was experiencing delays and manager dissatisfaction with its hiring process, despite a staffing process that was doing a good job in providing ample applicants and keeping cost-per-hire low. An analysis of the reasons for these issues revealed that an ineffective recruiter and hiring manager relationship existed due to inadequacies by both parties. These include unrealistic hiring expectations relative to the market by hiring managers, and a lack of knowledge about the business and poor consulting skills among the recruiters. To address these issues, Coors redesigned its recruiting process and introduced revised performance goals for its "talent champions." Each performance goal included sample metrics to measure its achievement, and the metrics utilized included manager satisfaction scores and quality of talent. Coors recognized the importance of measuring what matters, and established one of the performance goals to utilize metrics to communicate how talent acquisition strategies help meet business goals.

Recruiting Cost Ratio

Perhaps one of the oldest and most frequently used metric to measure staffing efficiency is cost-per-hire. The standard cost-per-hire is the ratio of recruiting costs to hires, using number of hires as a measure of productivity. Simply put, a lower cost-per-hire implies a more efficient or productive operation, since more hires are obtained at a lower cost. Although widely used by many staffing organizations, cost-per-hire is not an accurate metric and therefore, organizations should not measure it. Before Staffing.org's 2000 Staffing Performance Survey, this standard had been largely unquestioned. Since then however, more and more companies have taken a harder look at cost-per-hire. Listed below are some of the inherent problems with this metric.

Geographic differences. Recruiting costs vary from one region to another. This is evident from the variances in labor markets, cost of living, and cost of services. A $4,000 per hire figure in Connecticut may reflect a highly efficient operation, while a similar figure in South Carolina may reflect a costly hiring process. Therefore the cost-per-hire metric reveals little when comparing one region to another.

Industry differences. Experience tells us that some industries (such as high technology) have more difficulty attracting candidates. Therefore, variations in cost-per-hire from one organization to the next reveal nothing about the efficiencies of their respective staffing operations. An organization in an industry that historically has difficulty attracting candidates may have a cost-per-hire figure that's twice as high as an organization in another industry, but may in fact have a more efficient staffing operation. The cost-per-hire measure simply does not, by definition, account for variations in hiring difficulty by industry.

Functional differences. Just as a cost-per-hire measure does not account for variations in industries, it also fails to account for variations in the types of positions being filled. For example, it is easier and less costly to find an HR generalist than a patent attorney. Because of this difference, comparing on a cost-per-hire basis for these two fields can be very misleading. The cost-per-hire metric does not help organizations that hire into a variety of fields understand the value or effectiveness of their staffing operations. Many, if not all organizations face this dilemma.

Differences in job levels. Compensation, of course, varies by level in each organization. As with the other differences, measuring on a cost-per-hire basis does not allow comparisons between different positions at different levels.

As such, the traditional cost-per-hire metric does not help organizations understand the value or effectiveness of their staffing operation. Recruiting Cost Ratio however, addresses these concerns. Recruiting Cost Ratio is superior to the traditional cost-per-hire metric when analyzing performance. RCR is an incredibly accurate and useful tool for budgeting and recruiting resource allocation.

To demonstrate how the RCR can be used to identify meaningful differences that a traditional cost-per-metric would miss, Table 8.1, taken from the 2005–2006 Recruiting Metrics and Performance Benchmark Report, uses a hypothetical example to compare both measures. Notice that although a higher cost-per-hire is observed for hiring radiologists compared to accountants, the staffing function is actually less costly in hiring radiologists since a lower RCR denotes fewer dollars spent for the function.

Organizations that use RCR, as opposed to the alternative cost-per-hire, will be left with a much more accurate portrayal of how efficient their recruiting operations are. The RCR is used to deter-

Table 8.1

| Type of Position | Total Staffing Costs | Total Compensation Recruited | | Traditional Cost-per-Hire | Recruiting Cost Ratio (RCR) |
		Positions Filled	Average Compensation		
Accountant	$ 60,000	10	$40,000	$6,000	15%
Engineer	$600,000	100	$60,000	$6,000	10%
Radiologist (Macon, GA)	$ 56,000	8	$70,000	$7,000	10%
Radiologist (New York, NY)	$140,000	20	$100,000	$7,000	7%

mine average HR spending on recruiting activities in relation to the starting compensation of new hires (positions filled) that result from staffing activities. To calculate RCR, follow these steps:

1. *Determine Total Staffing Costs.* Total Staffing Costs for a given period of time (usually one year) include all expenses associated with recruiting and hiring and are divided into four categories. Perhaps as important as the classifications themselves is the process of calculating each area separately as a percentage of compensation recruited. This promotes more accurate analysis of staffing operations and allows organizations that do not incur expenses in all categories to compare their performance to organizations that do incur expenses in all categories. Total Staffing Costs is the sum of the following expenses:

   • *Total Internal Recruiting Expenses.* This number is often referred to as "fixed operating expenses" or "internal or contracted expenses." It includes expenses incurred regardless of whether or not an individual was actually recruited. These are the fixed operating and maintenance costs of the recruiting function, from salaries and benefits for recruiting staff to office and technology expenses.

- *Total External Recruiting Expenses.* These costs, also known as "sourcing costs," include all external expenses which are incurred to specifically identify candidates. External expenses include fees for advertising, agency and search fees, costs associated with Internet postings, and virtually all other expenses incurred to identify and recruit candidates. External costs are typically not incurred unless there are specific positions to fill.

2. *Determine the Total Compensation Recruited (TCR).* This is the sum of the base salaries for external hires during their first year. Part-time employees working on an hourly basis should be included in this number. To process TCR for part-timers, simply multiply their starting hourly wage by the number of hours they were expected to work over the first year.

3. *Calculate the Recruiting Cost Ratio.* RCR = TCR/Total Staffing Costs. When multiplied by 100, the result yields a percentage. The percentage indicates how many recruiting dollars an organization spends for every dollar in new hire compensation.

Recruiting Efficiency

It is imperative to understand the distinction between Recruiting Cost Ratio and Recruiting Efficiency. The two concepts, though similar, should not be confused or used interchangeably. While RCR should be applied solely for budgeting and resource allocation, Recruiting Efficiency is a comparison tool—the best measure of recruiting efficiency across function, industry, geographic area, and organization size. To calculate Recruiting Efficiency, simply subtract the RCR from 1. This operation inverses the RCR and yields a percentage relative to 100; the higher the percentage, the more efficient the recruiting function. And because Recruiting Efficiency is a derivative of RCR, it calculates what cost-per-hire misses and provides a standard way to compare recruiting efficiency across positions.

Case Study: Measuring New Hire Quality

The challenges of recruiting metrics may be best examined by understanding the dynamics of New Hire Quality. New Hire Quality is the essence of recruiting and measuring; it is as daunting as climbing Mount Everest. And just like taking on Everest, the very people who encourage us to climb it, question whether it is really possible. This is the way of all great challenges. By gaining a clearer picture of New Hire Quality, it is quite possible to take away these lessons and apply these principles to other metrics.

Four years ago less than 2 percent of the companies in the United States were making any attempt to measure new hire quality. By 2002 that had edged up toward 10 percent, still a very small and inexcusable proportion for such a critical measure. And then by the spring of 2006 the total was approaching 40 percent. There is still more talk than measurement, but the talk is getting more serious and is coming from more senior levels. "Can you measure the quality of our hires?" is one of the top three questions the CFOs, COOs, and CEOs ask us every week. (The other two are how to measure HR performance and how to select HR vendors.)

WHY HASN'T IT BEEN MEASURED

While everyone agrees that new hire quality is important, many in HR question whether it can be measured. They are unequivocally wrong. New hire quality can be measured and any recruiting operation that is not doing so is inadequate at best. That said, it is important to understand why we haven't been measuring it. We're all professionals doing incredibly hard and complicated work that demands more, better, faster, and often with fewer resources. Metrics haven't been part and parcel of our work because there haven't been well founded and accepted standards regarding what we should measure or what the associated formulations should be. Collecting data is problematic and if we have the data, how are the results reported—what, when, and to whom? Consultants have also exacerbated the measurement of HR metrics. By definition, consultants are proprietary, and proprietary means they have to be different. So every consultant has different metrics to espouse. You can't and shouldn't embrace them all—what is a recruiter to do?

Quality is a particularly difficult metric because you have to decide when to take the measure and to differentiate impact of hires from employees in the existing work unit.

This further complication in measuring quality is the result of trying to assess the cause of quality performance. For example, is quality performance determined by the personal attributes of the individual or by environmental factors in the workplace? If the answer is both, then what are the relative contributions of each? The environmental factors in the workplace are clearly beyond the control of staffing operations, but they always make an impact, fairly or unfairly, on the perception of staffing's ability to deliver New Hire Quality.

There are two elements to evaluating new hire quality: What is it and when do you measure it?

What is it? The customer is the ultimate arbiter of any definition of quality and this includes new hires. Most of us have learned that the "I'll know it when I see it" approach to interviewing is ineffective and that clear requirements should be established before starting to source candidates. Defining new hire quality is just an extension of good recruiting practices. In addition to candidate criteria, initial on the job performance standards should also be established before recruiting is initiated.

These standards should focus on the first outcomes or contributions associated with the position and provide the basis for determining the quality of the new hire. For a new pharmaceutical sales rep, the number of calls, physician feedback, and sales may define quality. We'd suggest that the quality of a newly hired recruiter be based on his or her initial efficiency, customer satisfaction, time, and the quality of hires.

Some organizations use the first performance appraisal to measure new hire quality. This can be effective if the organization recognizes that the results are to be used for two separate purposes. One is to measure the quality of the recruiting and drive continuous recruiting performance improvement. The other is to measure and develop the new employee's performance.

When to measure? If new hire quality is defined by initial performance outcomes, it can't be measured the first day and rarely the first week. When to measure is as important as the definition of new hire quality because it represents when the hiring manager expects the new employee to first start contributing. This time-to-contribute should also be established before recruiting is initiated, and it should be subsequent to the euphoria of the new hire honeymoon and before the organizational influence prevails.

Most of us have seen stellar new hires fail under bad managers or in bad organizations. That isn't necessarily the recruiter's fault. New hire quality should be based on the new hire's initial performance, not organization dynamics. In order to most accurately measure the quality of the new hire, the evaluation should take place before the organizational influences can overshadow the employee.

The quality of a new clerk can probably be ascertained within two to four weeks. However, it may take as much as a year to fairly evaluate the new hire quality of a regional marketing director or research scientist.

As with all other valid metrics, a quality measurement fosters high performance. Establishing both the initial performance standards and when those contributions are expected before starting to recruit fosters better recruiting performance.

GETTING STARTED

Next to measuring, consulting skills are the most important re-cruiting and HR expertise. Good consulting skills will enable you to get the customer to help you to help them.

Like customer satisfaction, the new hire quality metric cannot be defined by a specific formula. Instead, it should be defined mutually by both staffing and business stakeholders. Use consulting skills to contract and work with the hiring manager to define quality and when it is to be measured. Quality is the first and most important staffing metric, and as such should be first defined at the very begin-ning of the recruiting process. Begin with the end in mind: "How does the hiring manager want the candidate to be performing at a predetermined point in time?" New hire quality and when the mea-sure is to be taken must be determined before recruiting is initiated.

One way to assess New Hire Quality is by tracking:

- Formal performance ratings of new hires: Is the performance of new hires consistent with the specifications used to make the hire?

- Retention rate of highly rated new hires: Are the new hires arriving with a high profile and great expectations about their impact if they stay long enough to fulfill their promise?

- Sources of retained highly-rated new hires: Where are these hires coming from?

You might also gather other information, since the process for assessing the quality of staffing operations is not formulaic. If you track the data we suggest above, you will be able to determine:

- Whether your operations align with your business as evidenced by the success of your hires when they are actually on the job.

- Whether you are producing highly rated hires who are truly prepared to have the impact on the business that they are expected to have (that is, are you hiring people who have the qualifications necessary to be successful in your system, or are you simply matching resume entries with job specifications?).

Often it is easier to initiate a metric if you assess prior performance. A simple associated strategy would be to ask hiring managers to review the criteria established prior to hiring and rate the new employee(s) today on a scale from 1 to 5. Possible criteria include:

- Goals.
- System compatibility.
- Capacity.
- Motivation.
- Knowledge and skills.
- Performance.
- Experience.
- Customer compatibility.
- Work group compatibility.
- Organization compatibility.
- Change/learning posture.
- Development areas.

Another approach is to ask the hiring manager to review each expectation listed and, on a scale of 1 to 5, assess how close the new hires came to meeting each expectation. Then the hiring manager can use these numbers to select a number, which reflects the overall quality of the new hires.

Whether or not you start measuring new hire quality by measuring prior recruiting activity, the most accurate measures require that new hire quality and the time to measure be established before recruiting is initiated.

Beyond Hiring—Metrics for Employee Development and Retention

Introduction

The overwhelming demands that the financial community places on Human Resources to demonstrate its accountability have launched the evolution of staffing performance metrics. Staffing has attracted attention, particularly over the past several years, because of increasingly larger amounts of money being spent to recruit employees. But when vast amounts of money are spent to attract new hires, there is serious pressure to hold on to them.

A significant part of Human Resources's response to the need to retain employees has been development, in all of its forms—training, mentoring, conferences, and attendance at high profile "executive programs." Because it costs a lot to recruit employees, it becomes reasonable to spend more to develop them; therefore, the same return-on-investment scrutiny senior management imposes on staffing operations is transferred to development. This is why assessing development and retention has emerged as a critical concern.

DEFINING DEVELOPMENT

Development is commonly used to describe almost any activity designed to improve an employee. This includes formal training, funding for continuing education, on-the-job training, and self-directed training. A viable definition of development is required in order to be able to measure it, but in order to define development we must first consider a few fundamental concepts.

PURPOSE OF DEVELOPMENT

Development can be thought of as having two purposes: to increase knowledge or to increase skills expertise. Traditionally, development activities have focused on increasing knowledge. The 1990s saw a strong movement to more closely connect development activities with performance outcomes, thereby refocusing on increasing knowledge in order to increase skills and expertise.

PERFORMANCE OUTCOMES

Development within organizations is not development for development's sake. Every development activity within an organization should result in eventual performance improvement. If not, then the organization should not invest resources in that development activity.

GENERAL VERSUS JOB SPECIFIC DEVELOPMENT

Human capital economists divide development into two categories: general and job specific. General knowledge development is typified by broad-based training programs, addressing general management skills (such as Coaching for Success or Keys to Negotiation), and it might include tuition reimbursement for completion of an undergraduate degree. While these types of programs are expected to increase job performance over time, most are frequently offered on a general enrollment basis without a short-term expectation of return on investment.

On the other hand, job-specific knowledge development can include courses or training that address subjects such as Essential Aspects of Managed Care, or Loan Eligibility Determination. Examples of job specific development include instruction in how to use claims processing software or how to operate a forklift.

Because general knowledge and skill development do not produce immediate, visible returns on investment, as job specific development does, there is often less financial support for it. On the other hand, job specific development is often supported easily, but specific and unambiguous returns are expected, usually in the short term. Nevertheless, progressive companies have learned that general development often pays off over time, particularly for key employees.

TIME FRAME FOR OUTCOME

Another factor that must be considered when examining development is how soon outcomes will occur. Simply stated, will the development initiative address knowledge and skills needed by the organization currently or in the future? Shortsighted organizations focus only on development to meet current needs, which usually results in a "firefighting" development mentality. Others recognize that the organization must develop capacity to meet future needs and capitalize on market opportunities.

FORMAL VERSUS INFORMAL DEVELOPMENT

Traditionally, development metrics have focused on formal development activities, primarily training. However, at least as much, and often more, development in organizations occurs through informal learning activities. Some of these nontraining developmental programs include:

- On-the-job training (OJT).
- Coaching.
- Formal mentoring program.
- Self-directed learning.
- Job rotations.
- Project assignments.
- Computer-based training.
- Conference attendance.
- Tuition reimbursement.

As we shall see, programs like these present what might be the toughest challenge in measuring development.

Given these considerations, a viable definition of development can now be offered: *Development includes all activities in which employees and organizations engage to increase the competence and expertise of employees for the purpose of improving individual and organizational performance.*

Retention

Defining retention as the percentage of the total workforce who leave the organization every year can create misleading conclusions about an organization. For some time, the objective was to aim for the lowest possible turnover. Then came the movement to eliminate the bottom 20 percent of performers. However, in today's tight labor market, the concern has shifted to retaining employees as long as possible.

Like quality, retention is best understood in the context of an organization, since measuring retention out of context is of little value. If an organization reported that its 1999 retention rate was 85 percent for all employees, what does that mean? Is 85 percent good, bad, or indifferent? There is simply no way to tell without further insight into the organization's goals and business strategies. If the 1998 retention rate was 80 percent, did this organization improve or worsen in 1999? Again, without more information, it is impossible to know. The following questions must be addressed to place retention into a useable context:

- Who is leaving? Are clusters of employees accounting for your turnover? What is the level of employees who are leaving? Are they long-term or short-term employees? Do particular sections of your organization produce disproportionate turnover? Are those leaving among the employees you want to leave or vice versa?

- Why are they leaving? "More money" and "an exciting opportunity" are the most common answers when employees are asked the reason for their departure. Not only are these answers predictable, they are also safe. Who cannot understand the attraction of a higher income or increased opportunity? Because these answers are difficult to contradict, they are seldom challenged, and therefore may conceal the more relevant reasons that motivate employees to leave an organization.

Because the simultaneous change of both a job and an employer is a major life-altering event, people seldom undertake such a course of action lightly. How likely is it that someone would seriously disrupt his or her life for a 5 or 10 percent increase in income? Unfortunately, behind these standard answers lie the alienation, feelings of disenfranchisement, a sense of betrayal, perceived lack of appreciation and recognition, and physiological injuries that drive most employee turnover. To understand retention, you must first know the reasons behind why employees are leaving.

• Where are they going? Do your employees routinely benefit by leaving your organization? Are you training your competitors' workforce? Why do the people who fail in your organization succeed in another? Answering these questions requires clarity about business goals and strategies and the expected role of HR management in implementing these business strategies.

The answers to these questions lead to a viable definition of retention:

Retention is the degree to which an organization keeps the workers it wants to keep and loses the workers it does not want to keep.

Using this definition, percentages alone are meaningless. Instead, their meaning lies in their relationship to predetermined goals, whose definition requires advanced planning and close involvement of staffing and HR with business management.

Approaches to Development Metrics

Development defies measurement in many ways. Unlike staffing, development is a virtual kaleidoscope of activities, only a portion of which are under the control of the organization. Development ranges from the informal and nearly impossible to measure, when one employee teaches another how to do something, to the formal and easily measured activity of employees attending formal training. It would be easy to throw up our hands in frustration, claiming it can't be done. But organizations demand accountability, so it is incumbent upon us to think creatively to produce metrics that advance accountability for development, even if they are still imperfect.

There has been a variety of attempts to create development metrics. In this section, we review six different approaches to measuring development. For each approach, we discuss the metrics, present examples, and identify the shortcomings in each that have led us to create new metrics for widespread use.

The American Society for Training and Development Approach. Each year the American Society of Training and Development (ASTD) prepares a state of the industry report that provides a comprehensive overview of employer-provided training in the United States. This report provides organizations with important benchmarking information for training, learning, and performance improvement processes, practices, and services. In short, it's a snapshot of investments and expenditures made in training across organizations.

ASTD Metrics Analysis. Unquestionably, these key figures (such as total training expenditures as percent of payroll, percent of training-eligible employees trained, training-eligible employees to trainer ratio, and so on) provide interesting training-related information. Another significant benefit of these measures is that they are based on readily available data. For instance, the calculation of total training expenditures per training-eligible employee is quick and easy since both figures are usually readily available in most organizations. It is difficult to imagine a scenario in which an extensive data collection effort would be required to obtain the figures necessary to make any calculation in the ASTD metrics.

However, in many ways the shortcomings of these measures mirror the problems with cost-per-hire, the traditional staffing metric discussed in the last chapter. Consider training as a percent of payroll, which has traditionally been used as the key metric. What does it really mean? Is any manager using it to decide how much training to offer employees? Is any organization that makes strategic training decisions using it? While it is an interesting benchmark, it does not seem to be one that has led to increases in training budgets within organizations, even though training investments have increased.

Furthermore, because these metrics focus solely on training, their scope is entirely too limited to be used as effective development metrics. Other developmental programs and initiatives (such as OJT, coaching, mentoring, and so on) are not included, thereby leaving a tremendous void in their usefulness as developmental metrics. As noted earlier, development, unlike training, is not limited to structured learning activities designed to help employees fulfill job duties. Instead, it extends past training to include short- and long-term activities. Unless an organization has an extraordinarily good human resource accounting system, these activities are not likely to be included in training expenditures. The general trend in organizations today is to use more nontraining initiatives, making these metrics even less useful. By omitting or overlooking developmental efforts that extend beyond training initiatives, the ASTD metrics are incomplete and inadequate for our use.

The Human Resource Development Evaluation Approach. Training and human resource development professionals have taken a completely different approach to measuring development. Unlike the organization-level metrics employed in the ASTD approach, they have focused on intervention or program-level measures through what is typically called "evaluation." Under this approach, individual development interventions or programs are evaluated, and the results are aggregated to provide organization-level metrics.

There are two basic problems with this approach:

1. Extensive data collection efforts are required to evaluate enough programs to get organization accountability (history tells us people will not do this).
2. Comparison data across companies would be limited.

Therefore, the metrics approach presents an alternative to accountability. It is an easier approach and one more likely to be used. Program-level results assessment is very useful for diagnosis of programs, and while we support program-level results assessment, results have clearly shown that development of it does not fit our purpose (Swanson 1998). The persistent low levels of training evaluation, particularly at the more sophisticated levels three and four, raise serious questions about the state of training evaluation research as well as whether currently used models will enable trainers to achieve higher levels of program evaluation. Simply stated, in 40 years of promoting, its use has not changed the overall picture; something else must be needed.

The Financial Approach. Traditionally, Human Resources has not looked to Finance and Accounting to create metrics. While it will become clear that metrics other than financial ones will be needed, this separation between Human Resources and Finance is unnecessary and counterproductive. Thus, we will consider some basic financial metrics to inform our new development metrics.

The financial approach represents selected financial metrics related to development that have arisen from human capital economics, utility analysis from industrial-organizational psychologists, intellectual capital, and financial analysis. The financial approach has been to use existing financial measures to place value on human capital.

Intellectual capital theory posits that some employees are more productive than others due in large part to their acquired knowledge, skills, and abilities. The presumption is that returns from human capital are represented by the difference between the worth of a firm's assets and the value placed on it by the stock market.

An example of this approach is the Human Capital Return Metric. Intellectual capital theory has attempted to use financial measures to determine the return from human capital. One key metric for human capital is the following:

$$\text{Human Capital Return} = \text{Market Value} - \text{Book Value}$$

From this perspective all returns over the book value of the firm are attributable in returns from human capital development. However, book value is often too conservative, so another approach is to use Tobin's Q, which is:

$$\text{Human Capital Return} = \frac{\text{Market Value}}{\text{Replacement Cost of Assets}}$$

This ratio controls different depreciation policies that affect book value. Values greater than one indicate returns from intellectual capital.

Intellectual capital theory is fundamental to any attempt to create development metrics; however, the use of market value to calculate human capital returns is problematic except in the long run. We need only look to the stock market in the late 1990s (particularly Internet stocks) to see how market valuations can become disconnected from real firm performance. Thus, linking development metrics to stock market valuations could create tremendous short-term volatility in the metric, rendering it unusable.

Human Resources/Performance Research Approach. There has been a flurry of research in recent years linking Human Resource best practices to organizational performance. Research suggests that human resources do make a difference. There are several core premises underlying the performance approach to Human Resources:

- Performance-based Human Resources must enhance current performance and build capacity for future performance.
- Training and other development initiatives cannot be separated from other parts of the performance system.
- Effective performance systems are rewarding both on an individual level and an organizational level.

Given these assumptions, it is easy to understand why the interest in human resource and performance research spans many disciplines from psychology to sociology to HR management and many others. Like the ASTD approach, the human resources and performance research approach is typically an organizational-level approach using broad metrics of Human Resources practices.

The direct correlation of these metrics with performance strengthens the case for creating metrics to measure development. These studies provide clear evidence that development (and other Human Resource activities) is related to performance.

However, while some measures of Human Resource activity have worked, most rely on information that is not readily available. Most use special surveys, some of which are labor intensive. In addition, as a practical matter, these metrics are generally not easy to attain, and are therefore not considered to be optimal or practical as our development metrics.

Human Resources Metrics Approach. We are certainly not the first to consider that new sets of organization-level metrics are needed. We will call this the Human Resource metrics approach, which includes work by Fitz-enz, Ulrich, Zenger, Smallwood, and Kaplan and Norton. In general, these researchers have adopted a similar approach to ours. That is, they have attempted to define key organization-level indicators that provide a picture of development effectiveness across a broad sample of companies. These metrics examine the following areas:

- Lagging indicators.
- Leading indicators.
- Collective assessment and quantitative collection measures.
- Employee competence.
- Learning and growth perspectives in terms of employee capabilities.

These metrics, without a doubt, are most directly associated with our goal of identifying or establishing development metrics. They also clearly demonstrate the value of organization-level metrics used in a balanced scorecard approach to HR accountability. Together they provide a useful starting point. However, they have enough flaws that we are reluctant to adopt any of them entirely. There are two primary flaws:

1. They still tend to rely heavily on training as a key indicator (not on our broader conception of development).
2. Some are too complex to collect in large-scale surveys such as ours. For example, establishing employees' reputation with headhunters would be a difficult task.

Development and Retention Metrics: Getting Started

Assessing retention and development (how do you do it, how much do you assess, where do you begin, how much of the organization do you include, and so on) can be particularly difficult. The questions are endless and the temptation arises to make a declaration that development, of course, is good for people, so it must be good for the organization. However tempting and rational this argument may seem, HR simply must have more accountability today. And, while the idea that development is "good for people" is not enough, the process of assessment cannot be so overwhelming that it often gets pushed aside.

As the preceding discussion illustrates, a variety of metrics are being offered today. As we set out to review existing metrics and draft a useful set of new metrics, we used these key criteria:

- Parsimonious: Limiting the number of key criteria instead of using a lengthy scorecard.

- Usable by all companies: While we endorse creating company-specific metrics and scorecards, for the purposes of this book, the metrics should be applicable to all companies.

- Provide leading and lag indicators: Leading indicators predict future performance while lag indicators report on past performance. Leading indicators are especially important because they provide management with early warning signs of future problems.

- Balance new data with existing data: While it's easy to create metrics that require entirely new information systems, it's not practical. The most effective method is to create metrics that incorporate some existing and easily accessible data with new data.

- Useful to management: As seen from the HRD approach to measurement, metrics that are not useful to management are not likely to be completed.

- Correlated with performance: The metrics should have a reasonable chance of predicting performance.

- Not easily manipulated: The metrics need to be credible and not easily manipulated.

- Based on systematic information: Too often, development metrics are based on anecdotal information. The best metrics provide hard data.
- Minimally impacted by extraneous factors: The metric must reasonably represent organizational factors without incorporating unrelated extraneous factors.

Proposed Development Metrics

In this section, we present our proposed metrics for development. Development metrics are among the most difficult to create. Staffing and retention metrics have a well-defined focus and a limited group of employees to examine. Therefore, it is possible to calculate fairly precise measures. Development, on the other hand, represents an enormously diverse array of activities, many of which are not accounted for or tabulated in any information system. Furthermore, they must include every employee every year, not just a subset, such as those who leave or stay.

Our review suggests that development metrics could be created at three levels:

- Organization or organization sub-unit level.
- Intervention or program level.
- Individual employee level.

We have opted to create organization or sub-unit metrics rather than intervention or individual level metrics. Our rationale is simple: After 40 years of failure to establish intervention or individual-level measures as a viable accountability system, we see little reason to recommend them now. They are not likely to succeed. Some organizations certainly may do them, and may have wonderfully valid data that we applaud. But our interest is in broadly applicable metrics, so we have chosen a different direction.

Metric One: Development Quality. One of the chief goals of development is to have people ready to fill vacancies as needed. An appropriate metric of development quality is the percentage of vacancies that the organization can fill internally. It is important to keep in mind that this metric is not intended to suggest that all vacancies should be filled internally, but rather that they could be because development is effectively preparing employees to take on new responsibilities. Also, in instances where new hires are used to replace those who leave or those positions emptied due to the internal hire's promotion, it is necessary to subtract these vacancies since they represent an expanded job base. Finally, there will be positions that the organization decides to fill externally. Thus, the metric should be presented as a percentage of vacancies only in situations where the desire exists to fill internally. With that in mind, the ideal situation is one where organizations fill 100 percent of the positions (that management wishes to fill internally) internally.

$$\text{Development Quality} = \frac{\text{\% of Vacancies Filled Internally with Qualified People}}{\text{\% of Vacancies Desired to Be Filled Internally}}$$

Metric Two: Capacity to Meet Potential Needs. Capacity metrics provide an assessment of the organization's ability to meet future needs for innovation, problem solving, and growth driven by human capital in the future. The premise of Capacity to Meet Potential Needs is that there is substantial cost to any organization that does not develop people in advance of the roles they must assume. The cost may occur because an employee leaves, with nobody qualified to fill the position, resulting in lost productivity and perhaps costs to recruit externally when it is not desirable. Another negative scenario occurs because growth opportunities requiring quick action by the organization present themselves, leading to opportunity costs if capacity is not present.

We believe these situations are best combated by two metrics. Before this can be addressed, however, an organization needs to have a reliable, flexible and mobile workforce. That is, it is possible for an organization to have only just enough competent employees to meet current demand, but not an excess that could be utilized should the need arise. Thus, we propose using the following metric:

$$\frac{\text{Capacity to Meet}}{\text{Potential Needs}} = \frac{\begin{array}{c}\text{\% of Key Positions with at Least}\\ \text{One Internal Employee Also}\\ \text{Qualified for Position}\end{array}}{\begin{array}{c}\text{\% of Key Positions Desired}\\ \text{to Be Filled Internally}\end{array}}$$

Capacity is built by a certain degree of over-investment in development so that more than one person can fill a position. This metric requires an organization to determine which positions are essential to the organization's business and success. These should be positions that are deemed critical to the organization's future. Also, how many of these key positions should be filled internally? The final element that must be examined is the number of key positions that have at least one additional employee suitable to fill the position if necessary. This data plays a dual role—both in calculating the metric and by forcing the organization to examine its succession planning procedures. Capacity also depends on an employee's motivation to use learning and development to enhance performance. Traditionally, this has been stated as motivation to learn. However, given that the primary desired outcome of organizational development programs is improvement in work outcomes, an exclusive focus on motivation to learn or train is too limiting. The process of improving work through learning also involves an employee's willingness to transfer knowledge acquired to improve work processes. Thus, motivation to learn is a necessary but not sufficient condition for successful development.

To address this, a new metric is recommended: Employee Motivation to Improve Work Through Learning (MTIWL). This metric posits that an individual's motivation to improve work through learning is a function of his or her motivation to train and motivation to transfer, symbolically:

$$\text{MTIWL} = \text{Motivation to Train} + \text{Motivation to Transfer}$$

Because organizations have an appropriate interest in something more than just "learning for learning's sake," the MTIWL construct focuses on motivational influences that will lead to improved work outcomes from training.

Metric Three: Development Customer Satisfaction. Perceptual data is inherently flawed due to its subjectivity. Nevertheless, customer satisfaction is an important aspect and should not be limited to only recruiting metrics. Unlike most development satisfaction data, this book recommends adopting the Results Assessment System's approach for two reasons. First, there is an established need to collect perceptual data from the manager's standpoint of development participants rather than of the participants themselves. While participants may be consumers of development, it is their managers who are the true customers. Second, the perceptual data to be collected focuses on utility of development for improving performance. Typical perceptual data asks how much participants like development activity. Research has consistently shown that this has no relationship to learning or performance outcomes. The appropriate measure is utility of development for improving performance. The recommended metric should be: Average Manager Rating of Training and Development Utility for Improving Performance.

Metric Four: Formal Development Investment per Employee. Traditionally, training investments have been measured by training expense as a percent of payroll, but this measure is flawed for a variety of reasons. The improved metric—Formal Development Investment per Employee—takes a more holistic approach and considers the following:

- Expanding beyond training cost to include other formal development.
- Including the hidden cost of the participant's salary.
- Converting to a per person ratio so it is more usable by management. We acknowledge one key shortcoming in that it does not include the cost of informal development, which is simply too difficult to cost. The metric is calculated as follows:
    - Internal Costs (IC) = training expenses + direct costs of learning events
    - External Costs (EC) = tuition reimbursement + conference registration fees + outsourcing + other development costs
    - Hidden Cost (HC) = (participant days in training + conference days attended) × average payroll per day
    - Formal Development Cost (FDC) = IC + EC + HC
    - Formal Development Investment = FDC/FTE

Metric Five: Human Capital Development Contribution (HCDC). While some claim that the value of development cannot be precisely calculated, HCDC is the measure that comes closest to anything we have seen. As stated earlier, in the financial world economic value added, or EVA, has become a popular way to value business units. EVA is simply the profit attributable to a business unit less the cost of capital employed in that unit. Fitz-enz (2000) proposed a measure he called human capital value added (HCVA), which he defined as revenues minus expenses except for pay and benefits, divided by number of full-time employees (FTEs). Unfortunately, this value is flawed in that it attributes all profit to human capital and ignores the role of financial capital. This new metric, Human Capital Development Contribution, is calculated as follows:

1. Calculate Economic Value Added (EVA) for the operating unit as:

$$EVA = \text{Revenues} - \text{Operating Expenses} - \text{Cost of Capital}$$

   In most organizations, a good estimate of the cost of capital can be easily obtained from the Finance department, particularly for the entire company.

2. Next, calculate the Human Capital Contribution Percentage. In EVA, the cost of capital is considered the cost of financial capital. Thus, the cost of human capital is total compensation. HCCP is then defined as the ratio of total compensation to the sum of total compensation and the cost of capital.

$$\text{Human Capital Contribution Percentage (HCCP)} = \frac{\text{Total Compensation}}{\text{Total Compensation} + \text{Cost of Capital}}$$

3. Calculate the returns attributable to human capital by multiplying EVA by HCCP. Then, divide by total compensation to estimate value added per dollar of compensation as follows:

$$\text{Human Capital Development Contribution} = \frac{EVA \times HCCP}{\text{Total Compensation}}$$

4. Calculate development as the year-to-year change in the HCDC.

Approaches to Retention Metrics

The days of spending an entire career within a single organization have long since passed, particularly within large organizations or dynamic dependent industries. This affects both younger and older employees, although older ones are known to be more stable. Thus, any discussion of retention naturally involves a discussion of turnover and measures of turnover.

The retention of human capital is a critical and never ending challenge for organizations everywhere. In the United States there are four common responses to the retention dilemma:

- Obsessing over turnover.
- Limiting internal job mobility.
- No rehires.
- Employee development.

Let's look at each of these and also review why these responses may or may not have any impact on retaining human capital.

OBSESSING OVER TURNOVER

Late last year we informally surveyed organizations to see how they defined retention. Most considered retention to be the percentage of employees who did not leave within a given time period—which is the inverse of turnover. If that is how an organization defines retention, we can understand the intense focus on cutting turnover. But retention is not the inverse of turnover. Retention is keeping the people you want to keep. Analyzing every turnover statistic and mandating across-the-board turnover reductions could actually trigger the law of unintended consequences. How? Because obsessing over all turnover discourages managers from terminating employees who should be terminated. And in reality, it does nothing to retain employees who should be retained. Retaining the wrong employees discourages the best performers and may even prompt them to look for opportunities elsewhere.

LIMITING INTERNAL MOVEMENT

The two most common approaches to this strategy are to limit the number of positions an employee may post for within a given time period and to extend the amount of time an employee is required to stay in a position before being able to "post out."

It seems as if every organization has tried the first approach at least once. That may be because it also addresses the concern that some employees spend too much time looking for other positions. Typically this policy limits employees to posting or pursuing between 4 and 10 positions a year. While limiting employee posting may appear to help internal position retention, it is fraught with problems. For instance, what if the best match—for the employee and the company—opens up after the employee has used his or her posting limit? This practice frustrates employees, hobbles internal movement, and seems to foster exceptions becoming the norm— always a bad thing. And if some employees are spending too much time looking for other positions it's the responsibility of the hiring manager and HR to address it, not change the rules for everyone.

Countless hiring managers complain that having an employee in a position for just 6 to 12 months is not enough. "Just when I get them fully up to speed they're moving on," is a common refrain. In most cases we'd agree, but two years is also too long for most positions. Minimum time-in-position requirements are appropriate for both the organization and employees. But organizations must recognize that if they are too long, it may well prompt employees to leave the company. Six months may be appropriate for positions that require a minimal learning curve. One to a maximum of two years is appropriate for positions that require more time to optimize performance. HR and managers should also realize that policy shouldn't be used to compensate for bad practices. Managers and the organization should be doing what they can to make employees want to stay.

Instead of mandates limiting posting or long and rigid time in position requirements, we favor eliminating posting limitations and establishing minimum time in a position from six months to two years, based on the position, with equitable consideration for exceptions. Companies including Johnson & Johnson have documented that open and well-administered job posting programs enhance employee communications, development, and, retention.

NO REHIRES

This policy actually is based on two premises. First, a no rehire policy is a punitive measure to discourage resignations because employees know they can "never come back." Second, organizations that embrace this first premise also believe that if someone left once, they will leave again. In short, why rehire someone when you know they'll turn around and leave again? Interestingly enough, exceptions to these no rehire policies are very common in the organizations that have them, a situation that raises a rash of legal implications. And even in organizations that do not grant exceptions, there is no data indicating that a no rehire policy enhances retention. Organizations would do better by openly embracing departing, valuable employees and wishing them well. There is value in ex-employees speaking well of their experiences. Rehire turnover is actually slightly lower than the total employee population and should be considered on a case by case basis.

EMPLOYEE DEVELOPMENT

Organizations that proactively support professional development of employees recognize that it is a top priority for most workers. Development can also enhance company performance and institutional expertise. Some HR departments make a point of meeting with each employee at least once every 6 to 12 months to formally review development plans and progress. In addition to these one-on-one planning sessions, employee development may include on-site professional association and university programs. We've heard arguments that organizations that offer these development opportunities run the risk of preparing employees for other organizations. But we are convinced that the overall benefits to the company and its workforce warrant the costs. Professional development is consistently a top three (along with quality of work and co-workers) retention factor for critical employees. And the ROI, particularly for job related professional development, can be quick and significant. Employee development can also impact organizational *esprit de corps*.

Human capital is complex. Often, what seems like a logical solution to a problem may have implications in dissonance with the objective. After defining a problem and instituting a quick fix, it's best to completely understand the challenge and implications before implementing any real change.

Predictive Retention Metrics

Just as turnover measures provide a lens for reviewing organizational retention, predictive measures of retention also provide a wealth of meaningful information on the subject. Two particular measures most commonly used by researchers in the field—Commitment and Intent to Leave—are probably the most useful and meaningful within this category of organizational metrics.

ORGANIZATIONAL COMMITMENT

On the most basic level, organizational commitment refers to an attitude that represents an individual's identification with and attachment to the organization. Individuals with high levels of commitment consider themselves to be true members of the organization, and they more readily overlook minor sources of dissatisfaction associated with the organization. These individuals also see themselves as ongoing organizational members. On the other hand, individuals with lower levels of organizational commitment have a greater tendency to consider themselves to be outcasts or outsiders in the organization. They also express dissatisfaction and see their membership within the organization as short-term only (Moorhead and Griffin 1995).

INTENT TO LEAVE

Commitment has been linked to the intent to leave construct, a behavioral intention that is a strong indicator of actual turnover. This behavioral intention, when coupled with job attitudes and/or available alternatives, plays an important role in organizational turnover. In fact, research has indicated that the intent to leave construct is a better predictor of turnover than job satisfaction.

Intent to leave is also affected by many factors outside of the workplace. Employees can hold jobs that they do not like without any intention of terminating the employment relationship. For instance, family considerations may require an employee to remain within a certain geographic region where desirable jobs may be scarce. Yet, because the employee's primary life interest falls outside the realm of work, he or she may choose to remain in the undesirable job.

Given its significance, it's easy to understand why intent to leave has been used extensively as a predictive measure of turnover and retention. Intent to leave is typically measured through a single three-item scale on an attitude survey.

Proposed Retention Metrics

At the heart of our approach to retention metrics is the core premise that effective retention metrics require an organization to more carefully examine each incident of turnover. Gross measures of turnover and retention really say little about the quality of employees lost and retained. The following metrics address these concerns.

Metric One: Turnover Index. Each organization will need to maintain a database of persons leaving the organization and make several key ratings about each person who leaves. These ratings will comprise the turnover index and be used in other metrics as well. Table 9.1 shows the elements of the turnover index.

High scores on this index (which ranges from 4 to 20) indicate a person that the organization would not want to lose. A low score indicates a person whose loss was unavoidable, that is easily replaced, was performing badly, and had little potential—in other words, a desirable departure.

The Index score, between 4 and 20, sums up the individual's desirability. A low score indicates an employee who is very likely to

Table 9.1

Element	Score (1 to 5)
Reason for Departure: To what extent was the departure potentially avoidable?	5 being potentially avoidable
Replaceability: How difficult will it be to replace the leaver with someone at the same level of competence?	5 being very hard to replace
Performance: How well was this person performing at his or her job?	5 being high performer
Potential: How much potential did the person have to move to a position with greater responsibility?	5 being high potential
Index Score	Sum the four ratings

leave yet easily replaceable, a low performer with little potential. A high score indicates the exact opposite—the most desirable type of employee.

Metric Two: Adjusted Turnover Percentage. Simple turnover statistics tell little about the exact nature of the turnover. Nonetheless, turnover percentages have appeal as they are familiar, simple, and easy to communicate.

$$\text{Adjusted Turnover Percentage} = \frac{\substack{\text{Number of Employees Leaving} - \\ \text{Number of Employees Desirable} \\ \text{to Lose}}}{\substack{\text{Average Number of} \\ \text{Employees during Year}}}$$

Metric Three: New Employee Loss Metric. There are two particular areas of concern for which special metrics are needed. The first of these is covered by this metric—the loss of new employees soon after employment. There is substantial evidence that the quality of new employee development activities and the manner in which new employees are brought into an organization is a key determinant of new employee turnover. It is also a very costly phenomenon. This metric addresses a simple-adjusted turnover for new employees for each of their first three years of employment (see Table 9.2).

Metric Four: Competency Opportunity Metric. This metric extends the use of the Human Capital Development Contribution

Table 9.2

	Lost in 2005	Lost in 2004	Lost in 2003
Employees hired in 2005			
Employees hired in 2004			
Employees hired in 2003			

(HCDC) ratio proposed in the development metrics. The core premise of this metric is that the loss of more experienced employees who are replaced by less experienced employees results in a lost economic value added that is rarely calculated. You may recall that HCDC is expressed as the dollar return for a dollar of compensation. Our second premise parallels that of human capital economics and utility analysis that says that a conservative estimate of the economic value of an employee's competence is represented by the employee's salary. The Competence Opportunity Cost is attributable to turnover, or failing to retain employees. To calculate this metric, one more thing must be added to the data collected for each person who leaves. Specifically, calculate the difference between the salary of each person who leaves and that of the person's replacement.

Compensation Difference = Annual Compensation of Leaver
  − Annual Compensation of
  Replacement

The result will be the economic contribution forgone by having a less competent person in the position. A positive number is a cost to the organization while a negative number represents a net gain for the organization.

CHAPTER
10

Succession Planning and Internal Mobility

How does Human Resources link succession planning and internal mobility? What measures of internal mobility can help adjust the enterprise? What measures of succession planning can help identify risk areas?

What does a healthy organization look like in its internal mobility and succession planning goals? Does the executive team think of staff as a collection of employees engaged in their current job? Or, are they a labor market to be leveraged for long-term strategic advantage? How do your employees feel about their long-term prospects inside the company? How about the "A" players that managers are counting on to provide the bulk of your profits? Succession planning and internal mobility are important strategic functions within every organization. This chapter aims to answer these questions not only to help you better understand these concepts, but to show how they can be implemented and measured.

Measuring the dimensions of your Internal Mobility program allows the organization to make decisions on retaining top talent, on where future talent may organically appear, and perhaps on how to increase employee productivity. When creating measures for Internal Mobility, it's helpful to put it into a market framework.

The simple fact is that you already have an internal labor market within your organization (see Figure 10.1). There are suppliers of talent (employees), consumers of talent (current and future leaders), market makers (HR), and sometimes technology to automate the process of making matches between suppliers and consumers. There are even artificial barriers to entry, such as a hiring manager who prevents her staff from moving within the company. Put too many restrictions on your supply of talent (your staff) and they will seek out new companies. Put no rules into the movement of candidates, and the internal market is chaotic (just like a financial market).

It is this market metaphor that provides Human Resources with the tools to measure the performance of your Internal Mobility program in detail.

Measure a Program, Not a Policy. Before you decide to measure Internal Mobility, examine your current Internal Mobility environment. An Internal Mobility policy and a job posting should be a starting point and not the final destination of your Internal Mobility system. A simple Internal Mobility policy, without the assistance of education, technology support, and management support,

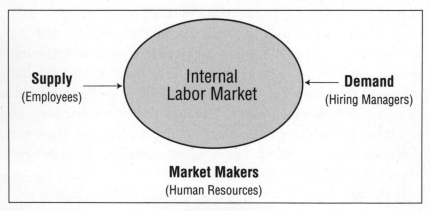

Figure 10.1

is not going to yield a healthy, mobile workforce. A fully supported program, however, is sustainable, measurable, and allows Human Resources and management to intervene, be nimble, and change to optimize the contribution of employees engaged in internal mobility. Optimally, the following would be part of a supported Internal Mobility program:

- *Management support and education.* Are there clear goals for what the Internal Mobility Program should accomplish? Can you measure to these goals? When new managers enter the organization, how are they introduced to Internal Mobility processes?

- *Technology.* If this is a labor market, how do you share information to make matches between employees and hiring managers? Internal Mobility systems should go beyond a job board and a form. It should assist your organization in managing employee requests, watching for good market behavior like managers reviewing and responding to employee applications, and so on.

- *Employee Career Path.* How are employees assisted in understanding the most frequent paths for their interests?

- *Succession Management.* Succession planning is usually applied to top management. However, who is managing the succession of the top five sales people in your hardest-to-hire areas? Succession management goals and processes can support that problem and round out an Internal Mobility program.

Case Study—Internal Mobility at Harrah's Entertainment

The following case study, which examines gaming giant Harrah's Entertainment, demonstrates how an organization can properly assess their talent and create an internal mobility structure based on solid, proven metrics.

Situation. In mid-2005, Harrah's Entertainment acquired Caesars Holdings, creating a combined Human Resources organization servicing the largest casino operator in the nation. With properties across the country, and several properties located in concentrated areas (Atlantic City, Las Vegas), it was clear to senior management that allowing their talent base to move freely across the organization was critical to keeping operating costs under control, recruiting costs minimized, and retaining talent in hard-to-hire markets like Las Vegas. Quite simply, for most locations where gambling is legal, a worker has more then one employer to choose from. Harrah's wanted to remain the choice of their well-performing employees even if their current job wasn't their final destination.

Support structure. To support their Internal Mobility efforts, Harrah's deployed:

- An executive-facing team to recruit and manage the careers of top casino managers across the country.

- A high-potential training and career development course for emerging entry-level managers to gain better visibility into their possible career choices. Partnering with recruiting teams nationwide to place high-potentials, they created personalized internal mobility assistance (with a champion within Learning and Development).

- An advanced, web-based internal mobility system. This technology included employee self-service in applying for new positions, and for checking on the status of all pending internal mobility applications. It also included level-of-service timers for Human Resources and for hiring managers in responding back to each other and to candidates on transfer requests.

The Internal Mobility Program in Action. For all employees, access is granted to an internal mobility system that is available at kiosks throughout the properties. Employees can not only apply for jobs, but also they can e-mail Human Resources about positions currently under consideration. Since each property may have different policies in accepting transfers, the system allows for location-specific policy management. Technology is used to make sure that employees are following the rules of the property at which they are interested in working.

Time-to-Contact throughout the Internal Mobility Process is a critical measure for Harrah's, so managers and Human Resources use technology to manage Time-to-Contact expectations as well, with flags indicating overdue tasks. See Figure 10.2, Human Resources Flags for Overdue Employee Activities (Hodes iQ).

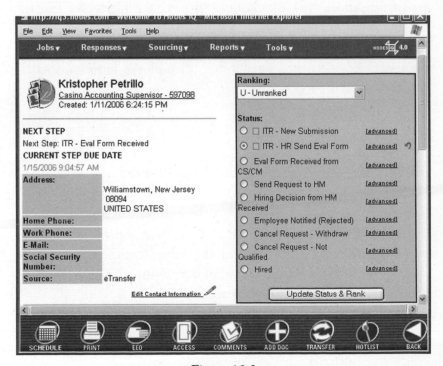

Figure 10.2

The system will flag for Human Resources when the next step is due and if it is overdue.

Leveraging the Program Using Metrics. Harrah's is able to capture all the information it needs for measuring Internal Mobility according to its goals through the use of systems and intensive education with Human Resources staff responsible for employee applications. The support systems used by Harrah's lay the foundation for reporting and allow it to create interventions where needed.

A Study in Tying Internal Mobility Directly to the Business. When disaster struck Louisiana in the form of Hurricane Katrina, the value of an embedded Internal Mobility Program was put directly to the test. With two locations entirely closed for months, Harrah's was able to leverage the technology and training adopted by Human Resources to manage thousands of displaced employees into properties across the United States within days. Harrah's CEO was able to announce its internal mobility emergency handling immediately through news outlets, and Human Resources was able to manage and report on a huge influx of employee requests, including accurate daily reporting to the CEO.

Measuring the Supply Side (Employees)

Retaining "A" players. Reducing voluntary turnover. Cross-training employees for better cooperation. These topics, usually discussed at executive meetings on the labor force, are, in and of themselves, cause to install measures to examine the health and attitudes of your internal mobility program.

Some Internal Mobility Program measures you already have in your hands can be used more effectively. Some are harder to create, but you likely have the data for it. Consider Table 10.1.

Table 10.1

Metric	Key Question
Percent of Internal Hires	Is your organization considering and hiring internal talent?
Employee Fluidity	How frequently do your employees move within the organization?
Measuring by A, B, C Players	Are your "A" players moving around the organization, learning the different businesses? Or are they being trapped by their department?
Termination Feedback	Are your voluntary terminations tracking whether they considered another job?
HR Time to Contact	Is HR contacting employees requesting transfers according to their service level?

METRIC ONE: PERCENT OF INTERNAL HIRES

Value. The Percent of Internal Hires metric can take advantage of data that you already have but may not have used as a management tool. Measuring the amount of internal transfers that occur is historically the first (and easiest) indicator to calculate. It will give an indicator of how likely an internal candidate will be considered for a position. This is the baseline figure that likely will predict employee attitudes to internal mobility and a culture of considering internal candidates first.

Depending on your business, the magic definition of what is a healthy number for the organization will vary. For example, in retail, most of the workforce may be entry-level, short-term employees. A healthy percentage of internal transfers is probably low. If you are a skill-oriented, intellectual capital focused organization, your fluidity number is likely high.

There are a few different ways of cutting the percentage-of-hires number, including: enterprise-wide, or by specific business area.

Audience. This is a basic statistic that is probably being examined monthly, which is appropriate. Assessing internal hires monthly or quarterly should be helpful when looking at the source of hire metrics.

When one tracks fluidity across the enterprise, one can assess the openness of the company to its own internal labor market. If the percentage of people hired internally is far lower than one would expect for the company type and size, then this data can be used to present new Internal Mobility policies to executives.

Data Elements. The data that you will need are:

- Total number of employees.
- Total number of internal transfer requests.
- Total number of internal transfers (hires).
- Total number of hires.

The Metric. Percent of internal hires = number of internal transfers/number of total hires

Presentation. This metric is simple to produce since it can be taken directly from source-of-hire data. Simply use your internal transfer hire data as the source data.

Comparing Against Goals. Finding meaning in the Percent of Internal Hires is tricky and should be judged against your company's goals. Organizations with a "promote from within strategy" but a low internal transfer percentage are probably out of sync with their business goals. After setting a baseline on these numbers, consider running the total number of internal applicants against the total number of hires at quarterly intervals to gauge how many employees were not chosen for the hires made in that time period. This may impact employee perceptions of how open the company is operating.

METRIC TWO: INTERNAL FLUIDITY

Internal Fluidity is also easy to calculate using data that you likely already have access to. Think of your internal labor as currency, the way that the stock market may think about a stock. The amount of trading of a stock in proportion to the overall number of shares is interesting to investors since it can tell you how much trading is really occurring within the market. The same idea applies to your employee base. You can literally measure how frequently your staff changes positions.

Value. The metric will examine how frequently employees move within the organization. This can help inform management on what growth is happening in the employee population and possibly on employee perceptions.

Audience. VP of Human Resources. This can be used as a management tool to assess the health of the Internal Mobility Program and what interventions may be needed. Key questions that the executive may ask are:

- Is this number too high or too low compared to total hires?

- Are our career pathing tools effective?

- Should fluidity be higher? Is the voluntary turnover rate showing talent leaving for lack of opportunity?

- If fluidity is too high: What intellectual capital leaves when an employee moves, and what systems can be put into place to retain their knowledge?

- If fluidity remains at its current level, what strategy should we adopt to grow employees and minimize voluntary turnover because of a lack of growth opportunities?

Data Elements. In order to calculate employee fluidity, you will need two pieces of data:

- Total number of internal hires.
- Total number of employees.

Fluidity is expressed as a percentage of total employees, so by dividing the total number of hires by the total number of employees, Internal Fluidity can be accurately assessed.

$$\text{Internal Fluidity} = \frac{\text{Total Number of Hires}}{\text{Total Number of Employees}}$$

Don't worry too much about the exact employee number to use (since the total number of employees likely changes weekly). You may wish to use the employee count as of the last day of the data that you have for the total number of hires.

Presentation. The Internal Fluidity number is presented as a percentage with commentary.

What if fluidity is too low? There are well-established recommendations for improving internal mobility, including employee career tracks, management versus experienced paths, and improving IT support of internal mobility. However, one problem area boils to the top of your internal mobility program: *Is your internal mobility program an open labor market?* If not, consider the blockers to an open labor market, and then open it to the point of pain. Employees join companies, and they leave hiring managers. Hiring managers may be too concerned that if employees leave their department the company will suffer. However, if the employees are going to leave and they are valued assets, then allowing them to leave to go to another part of the company is usually preferable. Managers stand to gain as well as lose from an open labor market. Training new managers on the benefits and costs of the open, fluid labor market is critical to success.

METRIC THREE: "HIGH POTENTIAL" MOBILITY

Managers and Human Resources both know who the high potential stars are. They probably have additional compensation consideration, may have been singled out for additional training, and more. How does your organization manage the career paths of these A players? A manager's preference is almost always to keep their star talent within their organization. But that might not be a healthy move for the organization if stars are turning over for lack of a career path.

Auditing career path plans for stars is, of course, essential. However, what kind of metric would assist an executive team in quickly assessing the mobility of your stars in the organization?

Simply enter the High Potential Mobility metric. By combining different pieces of data from performance reviews, voluntary turnover, and internal hire data, your Human Resources team can assess how the organization manages the career path of your stars. Star mobility provides a data point to the movement of the A players in your organization.

Value. The High Potential Mobility Metric provides Human Resources and executive teams with a summary statistic on the movements of their star performers. Use this statistic to focus the reader on your high potential employees to determine patterns—are your high potential employees moving about the organization the way you expect them to? Are they being promoted to new, higher-level positions? If not, then what can be done to address this situation? If human capital is truly an organization's most important asset, then management must take extra care to assure the retention of star performers. According to Staffing.org's 2006 *Recruiting Metrics and Performance Benchmark Report*, the lack of development opportunities is the single largest factor that employees cite for changing employers. Thus, it is critical to make these development opportunities readily available to star performers. In order to maximize the potential of your organization, it is imperative that you exploit all of your strengths, particularly with regard to human capital.

Audience. This metric may be of some interest to executives as a single summary statistic, and also to the vice president of Human Resources and likely the head of Learning and Development. The information you learn from it, however, has leverage points at the hiring manager level. If you see patterns of high potentials fleeing one particular manager, then senior management may need to explore the situation further.

Goal setting questions for this metric:

- How often should our star performers move within the organization to learn the business?
- Is there a percentage goal for lateral movement?
- Is there a percentage goal dictated by career paths?
- Are there warning signs for high potentials leaving that we can detect from this data?

Data Elements. The data that you will need. Note that there are three different "sub-metrics" within the High Potential Mobility metric.

Metric One: Percentage of High Potential Internal Hires. Simply examine the hires made within the time period, and take the percentage of the internal hires that were high-potentials. Use the formula below; multiply the figure by 100 to yield a percentage. This becomes your Percentage of High Potential Internal Hires. You will need the following data:

- The number of High Potential Internal Hires.
- The number of Total Internal Hires.

$$\text{High Potential Internal Hires Ratio} = \frac{\text{High Potential Internal Hires}}{\text{Total Internal Hires}}$$

Metric Two: High Potential Mobility. Data needed for a corporate-wide statistic:

- The total number of High Potentials.
- The total number of High Potentials hired for an internal job.

$$\text{High Potential Mobility} = \frac{\text{High Potentials hired for an internal job}}{\text{Total Hire Potentials}}$$

Metric Three: High Potential Voluntary Turnover. Since you already have voluntary turnover data, assessing the percentage of voluntary terminations that were high-potentials is an important statistic, even though the high-potential has already left. From this, you can assess if there is a global problem in managing career paths on high-potentials. You may want to consider looking at the results of the exit interview to understand your high potential voluntary terminations more closely.

The following data is necessary to compute this measurement. Of course, you may want to cut these statistics by division, branch, and so on.

- Total number of voluntary terminations.
- Total number of high potential voluntary terminations.

$$\frac{\text{High Potential}}{\text{Voluntary Turnover}} = \frac{\text{High Potential Voluntary Terminations}}{\text{Total Voluntary Terminations}}$$

Presentation. This type of analysis is best to calculate on an annual basis, and may not be important enough to include on an executive dashboard-type report. Initially, run this data for diagnostic purposes to see if there are red flags, then present them in working meetings on the topic. Table 10.2 provides an example of how to

Table 10.2

High Potential Data	Statistic	Commentary
% High Potential Internal Hires	6%	We are considering
High Potential Mobility	2%	Our high potentials may not feel like there is mobility when looking at peers.
High Potential Voluntary Turnover	26%	Turnover is too high for these employees. We are not hiring high-potentials fast enough to replace.
High Potentials Considered for Management	30%	70% of management jobs are either not-high potentials or externals—is this right for our organization?

present this data. Please note that the commentary provided is an example; whether your numbers are cause for intervention depends on your management goals.

You may need to drill down into the data to learn more about high potential movement, including hiring manager patterns. Do high potentials tend to leave one manager? Do high potentials tend to move to a specific manager? Are they being promoted or moved laterally? How do their moves map to typical career paths for that job? Is there anything we can learn to adjust the career path?

METRIC FOUR: EXIT INTERVIEW FEEDBACK

Since it's always helpful to leverage activities your organization is already engaged in, it's useful to gauge the sentiment and feedback during exit interviews on voluntary terminations. Most organizations have a program for exit interviews. No matter what your current state of the interview survey, there is likely another layer of interview information that the organization may need to improve processes in the future. If your exit interview survey focuses only on "reason for leaving," try drilling down into 180 degree management feedback. If you have a more mature program, try exploring other areas like training, development, and willingness of the enterprise to explore new ideas.

Value. Exit Interviews analyses are, at best, historic readings that can be mined for patterns. But beyond the reason for leaving and the percentage of voluntary turnover, few statistics are ever examined in the exit process. But there is valuable information to squeeze out of an exit interview.

Use exit interview data to examine attitudes towards internal mobility, both from the employee's standpoint and from the manager's standpoint as well. Are there good employees leaving because managers are holding them back?

Audience. Senior Managers.

Data elements. During the exit interview, you may want to add questions such as these into your survey:

- Did you consider an internal opportunity before you made your decision?
- Was your manager encouraging or discouraging you to explore other opportunities?
- Where do you hope your next position will take you on your ultimate career path?

Please note that if you use an electronic survey, it's much easier to compile this information.

METRIC FIVE: HUMAN RESOURCES TIME-TO-CONTACT

Follow-up on an employee transfer request is absolutely critical for Human Resources. The cost of not following up on an employee referral is well understood by most Human Resources managers, but sometimes not by the Human Resources staff, the prospective hiring manager, or new entrants. Lack of follow-up hurts the career prospects of an employee, hurts the manager looking to hire, and builds a reputation that the Human Resources department is unresponsive to their constituents. As a Human Resources staff management tool, measuring Time-to-Contact is suggested.

Value. Ensure that Human Resources and hiring managers are getting the simple things right. Are they contacting the employees that have applied for jobs? Is this within the contracted time-to-contact?

Audience. Human Resources staff and hiring managers responsible for contacting employees on internal transfers.

Data elements. Ideally, your applicant management system will allow you to track this, since routed communications are involved. What is needed is the date of initial employee request, the date of Human Resources contact to the employee, and the date of hiring manager response (where applicable). Take this data and average it across a month of internal transfer requests completed to determine the average time-to-contact. Compare this number with the contracted time-to-contact agreed upon by Human Resources members and (ideally) hiring managers.

Demand Side = Succession Planning

For most businesses, succession planning is an exercise reserved for the CEO and other C-level positions. Current best practices in the most expansive organizations have extended the planning process further down the management structure—senior management first, then through the organization levels two or three reporting levels, capturing more of the long-term planning needs for management in the organization. Measurement within succession planning has been virtually nonexistent. Having a plan in place, with buy-in from directors, was sufficient for Human Resources management to the executive level.

Depending on your organization's attitudes toward succession, succession planning could mean several things (Burke 2002). In order of level of effort, succession planning could mean the things shown in Table 10.3.

Admittedly, the idea of succession management may cross over into areas of workforce planning, learning, and development. However, the planning aspects of succession management cut to the heart of critical questions enabling a company to sustain and grow a competitive advantage. Among the questions to be addressed are:

- What positions have the greatest impacts on revenue growth and profitability?
- In those positions, what is the difference in contribution between an A player and a B or C player?
- Where is the organization vulnerable in these key areas if your top performer(s) leave?
- Who would succeed these employees?
- What kind of tools and training will they need to contribute efficiently?
- Special attention should be paid to a timely question: How will baby boomer retirements impact the business function?

Table 10.3

Replacement Management	Forecasting replacements and/or retirements. This has special urgency starting in 2008 with baby boomer retirement.
Succession Planning	Forecasting and staff development for the top areas.
Succession Management	Forecasting and staff development for all business areas.

We suggest that in the twenty-first century Human Resources organization, succession planning must be treated as the process closely aligned with succession management. The anticipated impact of the available labor pool combined with retirements (or semi-retirements) force the hand of Human Resources to plan farther ahead in building a workforce with sustainable human competitive advantage. It is through this lens that metrics have been suggested to assist management in making intelligent decisions on succession management of key positions. Some metrics are used to find vulnerable areas, others are used as tools to plan over the long term how to manage those vulnerabilities.

Managing Long-Term versus Short-Term Staffing. Any health care staffing manager understands the labor-force projections all too well—and looking at a graph of available nurses versus demand over the next 15 years proves the crisis in startling detail. There won't be enough experienced nurses to staff the demand by a huge margin. The health care market may provide a glimpse into our collective futures in staffing shortfalls—the chronic staffing need, reactive hiring, and constrained budgets.

It is well understood by staffing managers in health care that they are fighting a long-term staffing problem with short-term budgets. This may be the reality in all of our staffing futures. Without metrics and a clear expression of the future need, there is little hope of funding the long term problem.

METRIC ONE: VULNERABILITY SCAN

Value. Succession management is an exercise in forecasting future events. The Vulnerability Scan is a tool that can be used to measure the succession situation and identify the vulnerable areas of the organization. It will allow management to prioritize those areas that need attention.

This analysis should embed context into the report; managers can't make a decision on succession management in a department without having perspective into the business impacts, financials, and future anticipated need for the company.

Audience. Senior executives and impacted hiring managers.

Data elements. For each job title that you suspect has a succession risk to it, gather the following types of information:

- Job Title/Job Group. Group your at risk jobs into competencies or use single roles where appropriate.
- Strategic Impact. What type of job is being evaluated? High financial impact? Low? Sales? Management of a business line?
- Total number in title. What is the business impact of this position? Does it contribute disproportionately to revenue? To profits?
- Total number in cross-over titles. This is the total number of employees in a job title that is transferable into a job.
- Talent Depth. Gather information about potential successors to this job. How many A players are possible? B players? The goal is to get a basic assessment of bench strength for the position, which may help determine the overall exposure on the position.

Presentation. Use the grid shown in Table 10.4 as your initial assessment of vulnerable areas. This grid helps to set priorities for the Vulnerability Action Plan (Metric Two).

METRIC TWO: VULNERABILITY ACTION PLAN

Value. Succession management is an exercise in forecasting future events. The Vulnerability Scan is a tool that can be used both to measure the succession situation and also to offer management

Table 10.4

Job Title	Strategic Impact	Total No. in This Title	Total No. in Cross-over Titles	Talent Depth		
				A	B	C
Sales Manager, Specialist	High	32	5	0	1	3
EVP, Marketing	High	1	0	2	0	0
Product Manager, Data Center Software	Medium	1	3	0	2	2

direction on each succession issue. This analysis should embed context into the report; managers can't make a decision on succession management in a department without having perspective into the business impacts, financials, and future anticipated need for the company.

Audience. Senior executives and impacted hiring managers.

Data Elements. For each job title that you suspect has a succession risk to it, gather the following types of information:

- Job Title/Job Group. Group your at-risk jobs into competencies or use single roles where appropriate.
- Red flag determination. Is this job/job group considered imminent or important enough to warrant a red flag to executives?
- Business Impact. What is the business impact of this position? Does it contribute disproportionately to revenue? To profits?
- Talent depth (A,B,C). Gather information about potential successors to this job. How many A players are possible? B or C players? The goal is to get a basic assessment of bench strength for the position, which may help determine the overall exposure on the position.
- Time to Contribute. Once an A/B player took this position, how long would it take to contribute productively to the job?

- Action Plan. If there is exposure on the position, recommend actions to be taken by different teams including learning and development, Human Resources, hiring managers, mentors, and executive management.

Presentation. The presentation of this document should be easily read by all stakeholders and it should be clear who owns what follow-up items from the succession plan. The grid presented in Table 10.5 illustrates the type of metric/action plan format that is designed to bring all parties together on key vulnerabilities.

Metrics Three, Four, Five, and Six: Succession Planning and Baby Boomer Retirement

The Baby Boomer retirement wave that will begin in 2008 has placed companies in a situation they have not previously managed in the modern business cycle: mass retirements of highly skilled, knowledgeable workers at a huge rate. No industry has been spared this management hurdle, nor have government, hospitals, and so on. Ask any engineering firm where their next generation of engineers is coming from; or any nursing team at a hospital in the United States, and the problem is clearly outlined in their minds: Their most senior leaders and workers will shortly be unavailable to their organization. Enter, an evolved view of how to use succession planning.

Succession Planning Will Exist Only at the Highest Levels in the Organization. The plan can't reside in the desk drawer of the vice president of Human Resources, nor should it be the only topic of discussion at the annual managers' meeting before lunch is served. This plan should be taken as seriously as a product roll out, a new division being formed, or any other group initiative that the company must face. It's a cross functional plan as well, touching almost

Table 10.5

Job Title	*	Business Impact	Talent Depth			Time to Contribute	Action Plan	Deadline
			A	B	C			
Sales Manager, Specialist	*	The product line for this sales team contributes 15% of revenue, but 30% of profits in the business unit.	0	1	3	8 months	L&D: Steep learning curve in technical knowledge. Identify training for potentials. Recruiting: Build long-term relationships for an external talent pool where needed.	2007
EVP, Marketing		Driving force behind the new markets initiative.	2	0	0	3 months	HM: Mentorship on both potentials should continue.	Retirement: 2008
Product Manager, Data Center Software	*	The data center software team operates in a highly competitive environment, with quarterly upgrade cycles. Without this role in place, long-term contract revenue becomes at risk within 12 months.	0	2	2	12 months	HM: Assess staff on talent and mentor the potentials. Identify to HR potentials. L&D: Assess potentials for management skill training.	2010

every aspect and level of the organization from Learning and Development to Finance, throughout all levels of management to Human Resources and, of course, the employees themselves.

Certainly this retirement wave will provide ample opportunity for Human Resources to lead the company through a rough terrain of recruiting, employee development, and strategic management, and ultimately prove yet again the value that best-in-class Human Resources management can bring to long-term company competitiveness. The first set of metrics will begin with evaluating the depth of impact to the organization. We then move into tools to help build business strategy around anticipated impacts.

METRIC THREE: THE RETIREMENT FORECAST

A basic retirement forecast can stimulate discussion among impacted managers and executives.

Value. The timeline predicts the number of retirements in key positions by year through the next five to seven years. This will help to map areas of exposure over the time horizon and will be used to build action plans. Some of these job titles may not require any action plan while some may. This will give executives an opportunity to differentiate between those that need a formal plan and those that do not.

Data Elements
- Job titles of likely retirees.
- Number of retirees in that pool, by estimated year.

Gathering this data can be sensitive. This is hardly a question one should put in an e-mail survey to employees. You can gather this type of information from a few different places. If your organization has a formal career pathing process, then you may even have some indication of the employee's intentions. If not, this may also

Table 10.6

Job Level	Number of Predicted Retirements			
	2008–2009	2010–2012	2013–2016	2017–2018
Sales	80	10	5	6
Director	4	11	12	15
Senior Director	5	2	4	0
Vice President	2	4	0	2
President/C-Level	0	0	3	1

be the opportunity to have personal conversations with potential retirees concerning their future plans and their openness to options such as part-time job sharing, mentorship, and other innovative programs. This allows Human Resources to understand the full range of options.

Presentation. The presentation of this type of timeline in Table 10.6 is straightforward, with job levels being analyzed on each row and the years of anticipated retirements on each column. Since this is a forecast, the date ranges should reflect the level of forecasting that you are able to engage in (red flag areas are shaded as an example).

Please note that since this is an initial forecast, the measurement here should not try to editorialize on solutions. Presenting this type of data to management will spur their own reactions to the data.

METRIC FOUR: SCOPE OF RETIREMENT IMPACT

Another flavor of pure prediction gauges the impacts of retirement on a department or functional skill area. This is especially useful in those areas with large numbers of highly skilled workers in niche areas. It is probably not enough for planning to understand that the organization will need to replace 50 percent of their engineering staff. There are many types of engineers, and the re-tiring engineers may have a skill set that a different type of newer engineer could fill.

Value. Analyzing the scope of impact on your skill sets within the company may assist managers in deciding how to manage the retirement wave best, precisely understanding what types of skills need to be replaced.

Audience. Senior managers and executives

Data Elements. Skill sets analysis/job title analysis. From your audit of key vulnerable areas, pick out the most vulnerable of the following data:

- The total number of predicted retirements in that skill.
- The total number of employees (currently) in that skill.

The exact size of the employee base with a skill will of course vary. Since it's a forecast, there is no need to worry if you have no feel on what that job title/skill set will be staffed like in five years—it will not matter. Use current data to help give you the forecast.

Presentation. Presentation of this data can use a similar grid to the timeline (see Table 10.7). Where there are obvious red flag areas, it may be helpful to highlight them for managers to pick

Table 10.7

| Job Title/Skill Set | Percentage of Retirements in a Job Title | | | |
	Business Unit #1	Business Unit #2	Business Unit #3	Business Unit #4
Turbine Engineer	59%	10%	3%	35%
Aerospace Engineer	10%	5%	35%	2%
Chemical Engineer	25%	10%	60%	12%
Mergers & Acquisitions	15%	45%	13%	5%
Sales—Aerospace Division	80%	0%	2%	15%

out exactly in a large list of data (red flag areas are shaded as an example).

METRIC FIVE:
BUSINESS IMPACT ANALYSIS

Value. Building on the first two metrics, partnering with managers, one can place a financial and business analysis to the roles. This type of analysis may also be effective in justifying funding for Human Resources projects in staffing and developing talent in vulnerable areas.

Data Elements. Each row contains the job title that is vulnerable during the retirement wave. The Key Skills column outlines the skills that create value. Current Revenue Impacts measures the sensitivities of that job on revenue. The New Business Impacts of the position (exposure to new sales, support of sales, product development, and so on). Other implications are reserved for describing impacts on business without revenue.

Presentation. Present Table 10.8 as a grid of the core competencies, revenue impacts, and implications of the business impact during the next X years.

Table 10.8

Job Title	Key Skills	Current Revenue Impacts	New Business Impacts	Implications
Turbine Engineer				
Aerospace Engineer				
Chemical Engineer				
Mergers & Acquisitions				
Sales—Aerospace Division				

METRIC SIX:
RETIREMENT ACTION PLAN

Value. The Retirement Action plan is the summation of all of the consultation and manager feedback on how to handle any emergent retirement issues. This should be the final working document that is adjusted and managed throughout time on how to handle all retirement issues.

Data Elements. Each row contains a Job Title/Job Segment that the action plan is appropriate for. The row can represent anything from a large number of employees needing to be replaced, to a single individual needing an action plan around him.

Total FTE: This is total number of FTEs predicted in retirement.

Work Plan: The work plan outlines the division making up the gap within the retirement years. We have included some of the major categories including mentoring internal high-potentials, work share among retiring workers, extending the retirement talent, external hires, and any business process engineering and/or outsourcing opportunities.

Outcomes: This is a summary of the plan for each job title.

Owner: The owner that will be held accountable for implementing the plan.

Presentation. This presentation (Table 10.9) is a matrix with each row as a job title or job segment. The plan for each job title is presented on each line.

Table 10.9

Job Title/Skill	Total FTE	Work Plan (Number of FTE)				Outcomes	Owner	Budget
		Mentor	Ret. Work Share	Hire	BPR			
Turbine Engineers	36	21	5	10	0	College recruiting over the long term has been creating a new team of talented engineers for future projects. Some retiree work sharing will continue to mentor younger engineers for best practices and within quality assurance teams.	L&D and VP, Engineering	$250k
VP, Development	1	1	0	0	0	Planned retirement in 2009. Several high potentials are within the unit.	L&D	$ 10k
Mergers & Acquisitions	10	1	1	8	0	Management goals are moving this team into new skill areas. Hiring from the outside is desired to gain new skill sets.	Recruiting	$400k
VP, Specialty Sales	6	2	2	2	0	Several high-potentials from within each unit are potential successors. During interviews, several potential retirees expressed interest in job sharing and mentoring for the next 5 years, transitioning clients to other sales teams.	VP, Sales	$200k
Logistics	50	2	0	0	48	Unit manager has recommended outsourcing the unit to a logistics vendor. Begins in 14 months.	VP, Logistics	$400k

168

CHAPTER

11

Current Measurement Practices— Lessons from the Field

If we take in our hand any volume of divinity or school meta-physics, for instance, let us ask: does it contain any abstract reasoning concerning quantity or numbers? No. Does it contain any experimental reasoning concerning matter of fact or existence? No. Commit it then to the flames, for it can contain nothing but sophistry and illusion.

—David Hume, An Enquiry Concerning
Human Understanding

Introduction

In every industry we need to be able to ask, "What is the performance of X and how do we measure it?" For example, in terms of education we need to be able to ask the question, "What is the performance of a good school supposed to be and how do we measure it?" and "What is the performance of a good teacher supposed to be and how do we measure it?" In the Information Technology industry we need to be able to ask "What should the performance of technology be?" and "What should the performance of a programmer be and how should we measure it?" In the field of sports we need to be able to ask both, "What should the performance of a player be?" and "What should the performance of a good team be?" There is a variety of names for metrics across the market: metrics, statistics, indicators, criteria, and so on. All of these names amount to a numerical way of judging performance. This is indeed what Hume's sentiment comes to; without metrics we can say very little with certainty.

The main reason we need metrics is that we can't know how to improve if we don't have a benchmark of how we are doing today. However, we also need to be able to chart how we have been doing over the last few days, months, and years. Therefore, our metrics should be saved so that we can access them and conduct research with them in the future. By and large our metrics need to use industry-wide standards so that we can compare one firm or individual's performance with another person or firm's performance in that industry. And indeed, these last two points are two of Geri Stengel's Ten Tips for Measuring and Improving Performance, "Compare Yourself to the Competition" and "Conduct Research" (Stengel 2003). However, there is no way to compare your firm with other firms or to conduct research without reliable metrics. This chapter will discuss metrics as they are used in (1) baseball, (2) the government, (3) information technology, (4) education, and (5) crime. Using these examples will help us to get a little clearer on why metrics are so important and the differences between the right and wrong metrics.

Ultimately the goal of this chapter will be to use the metrics of other industries to find best practices for generating HR metrics. This will help ensure that human resources metrics truly serve the industry. In 1978 Jac Fitz-enz proposed that "human resources activities and their impact on the bottom line could—and should—be measured." He was the first to argue for the relevance of HR Metrics because human resources have "a real impact on the bottom line." (Caudron 2004) At the time, this idea seemed pretty crazy, whereas now it is a commonplace.

HR metrics allow us to talk about human resources with others in our department, in our firms, and outside our firms. As Jamie Barber writes, "Perhaps the most crucial advantage of a sound HR metrics program is that it enables HR to converse with senior management in the language of business. Operational decisions taken by HR are then based on cold, hard facts rather than gut feeling, the figures being used to back up business cases and requests for resource." (Barber 2004) However, now that HR metrics have come of age it is high time that we try to understand what differentiates good and bad metrics. After describing the performance metrics used in a variety of industries, I will conclude with a list of 10 lessons that should be adhered to when generating performance metrics.

What Makes a Good Metric?

Perhaps the most obvious metric is money. If we want the best of something, say the best wine or the best television or the best school, then one of the ways we go about finding this best thing is to find out which is the most expensive wine, the most expensive television, and the most expensive school. If we were to use this method in finding the best doctor we would find the most expensive doctor and conclude that he was the best doctor. That is, we would conclude that there was a correlation between the expense of X and X's quality (and this is after all what we want from any metric, a well established correlation between the metric and performance). However, there are many problems involved with correlating the expense of X and its quality. There are market failures and other distortions (such as government regulations and other perverse incentives). What these all come down to, however, is that using money as a metric doesn't work a lot of the time. A performance metric should measure an outcome associated with an objective. Money does not meet this standard. Therefore, other metrics must be generated and used, but in order to generate such metrics a more comprehensive framework is needed.

One such framework was created by Professor William Clark, of Harvard's Kennedy School of Government. His framework for assessing metrics is one in which we could say that all good metrics are "credible," "relevant," and "legitimate." He writes, "'Relevancy' as we use it, is meant to capture the perceived relevance or value of the assessment to particular groups who might employ it to promote any of the effects noted above. 'Credibility,' as we use it, is meant to capture the perceived authoritativeness or believability of the technical dimensions of the assessment process to particular constituencies, largely in the scientific community. 'Legitimacy,' as we use it, is meant to capture the perceived fairness and openness of the assessment process to particular constituencies, largely in the political community." (Clark 1999) I hope that all the metrics I discuss here will be credible, relevant, and legitimate. Unfortunately, they will not all turn out to have these important characteristics.

It is extremely important to choose metrics that actually measure the thing that you want them to. An example of not doing this would be to measure random things that are correlated with good performance but which are not actually associated with that performance. This is one of Nassim Nicholas Taleb's main points in his book *Fooled by Randomness*, where he writes, "[M]y income started to increase after I discovered my slight nearsightedness and started wearing glasses. Although glasses were not quite necessary, nor even useful, except for night driving, I kept them on my nose as I unconsciously acted as if I believed in the association between performance and glasses. To my brain such statistical association was as spurious as it can get." (Taleb 2005) If Taleb were to generate a metric that correlated wearing glasses with performance, it would not be an efficacious metric. One of Taleb's points in his recent book is that we are often fooled by randomness into believing that a metric is measuring performance when in reality it is only randomly correlated with performance.

Of course, many people in the business world have thought about how to generate metrics of performance and they have learned a great deal about how to generate metrics that actually measure performance. Business strategist Geri Stengel generated a list of Ten Tips for Measuring and Improving Performance. Most important on his list are that you should:

1. Define your goals. "Determine your measures for success. Make your goals challenging, but achievable."
2. Determine the metrics to measure your company's performance. "Compile a list of factors that are important in your industry."
3. Develop methods to collect and organize data. "Determine a process for tracking and reporting all relevant data. Report on trends that emerge from your findings on a regular basis."
4. Conduct research. "When you need specific information about your customers and prospects that doesn't exist, conduct your own primary research" (Stengel 2003).

In the examples that follow I will discuss the metrics of many fields that use many of these suggestions when generating their performance metrics.

A COMMON MISTAKE

When generating and using metrics, there are many mistakes that can be made. One of the most common is to mistake Performance Metrics for Diagnostic Measures. According to Dave Trimble, Performance Metrics "are high-level measures of what you are doing; that is, they assess your overall performance in the areas you are measuring," whereas Diagnostic Metrics "are measures that ascertain why a process is not performing up to expectations. They tend to be internally focused and are usually associated with internal process steps and inputs received from suppliers." (Trimble 1996) To understand why we are not performing up to expectations is to not understand how we are performing. That is, Diagnostic Metrics are internal, whereas Performance Metrics are external. However, the only way to generate accurate Diagnostic Metrics is to have accurate Performance Metrics. In the world of metrics we have to move from the outside in (this is a lesson similar to the one obtained from the field of baseball).

In remedying this mistake, four leading questions are asked (Trimble 1996):

1. Do the metrics make sense?
2. How do they compare with your existing metrics?
3. Do they form a complete set (that is, have you adequately covered the areas of time, quality, cost, and customer satisfaction)?
4. Do they reinforce the desired behavior?

Trimble's questions will aid us in our quest to understand metrics in a variety of industries with the further goal of understanding what makes a good metric. These questions will help us to distinguish between internal and external metrics, which will in turn, help us to gauge how we are actually doing. In the HR world in particular it is important to retain the distinction between internal and external metrics.

How Other Industries Measure

Baseball. Baseball is one of the industries that show us that we could be measuring the wrong indicators when we're looking to see either how we're doing now or how well we're going to do in the future. Such metrics could mean that we're focusing on talent as opposed to performance. Talent is ability or potential, but the focus should be on performance. When we generate metrics, we want to measure performance—how well we're doing, but not talent—how well we might do in the future. This is because we can only gauge how well we will do in the future by taking an honest account of how we're doing now.

This is one of the reasons why baseball is an industry in which the way performance is measured has come under fire. Measuring performance in baseball should be one of the easiest tasks out there. You have players who are batting against the same players on the same fields. This means that generating statistics in baseball is fairly simple. The problem, however, is that sometimes we don't know which statistics indicate future success and which do not. That is, we don't know which statistics are relevant.

Michael Lewis's hugely successful *Moneyball* took the question of which statistics are relevant in baseball head on. The central argument of *Moneyball* is that the metrics that baseball insiders (including players, managers, coaches, scouts, and the front office) have used over the past century have been flawed. In Lewis's words, "Traditional yardsticks of success for players and teams are fatally flawed" (Lewis 2004). Some of the statistics that Bill James, one of the heroes of the book, derides as irrelevant are 60-yard dash times, RBIs, and batting averages. James showed that on-base percentage and slugging percentage are better indicators of future success and that getting a hit is less important than avoiding an out. In the end, every play in baseball can be evaluated (meaning that it can be given a metric) according to how many runs it will statistically contribute. An example of this is that a strike on the second pitch of an at-bat may be worth −.75 runs. This new piece of information (available only because new managers are focusing on relevant metrics) might fly in the face of the conventional wisdom, which is why getting people to truly believe in Bill James's new managerial system was extremely difficult.

However, when managers of teams started listening to James it paid off. When the Oakland Athletics (with $55 million/year) implemented the *Moneyball* strategy, they became competitive with the New York Yankees (with $205 million/year). (Lewis 2004) The manager of the Oakland A's, Billy Beane, the real protagonist of *Moneyball*, was the one who turned the team around. When the conventional wisdom said that you needed buff hitters and pitchers, Beane realized he could use James's system of metrics to come up with a winning and affordable team. Talent (at least in baseball) sometimes gets in the way of performance (which should be the real goal of a baseball team's manager), but Beane found a way, using metrics, to turn the tide on this system. The *Moneyball* story shows us again that one of the keys to good metrics is that they be relevant to performance in the industry where they belong and not just generally appealing or shocking. It also shows that sometimes the results of performance metrics will be counter-intuitive, so it will take a lot to get people (especially managers) on board, but it is often worth the fight.

Government. Even the government uses metrics to guide it in its decision making processes. Currently employed government-wide is the Executive Branch Management Scorecard, which is "used to show both how well a department or agency is executing the management initiatives, and where it scores at a given point in time against the overall standards for success." (OMB 2001) Each agency is graded on whether they meet a number of criteria.

The Office of Management and Budget (OMB) "assesses agency 'progress' on a case by case basis against the deliverables and time lines established for the five initiatives that are agreed upon with each agency as follows:

- Green (Success): Implementation is proceeding according to plans agreed upon with the agencies.

- Yellow (Mixed Results): Some slippage or other issues requiring adjustment by the agency in order to achieve the initiative objectives on a timely basis.

- Red (Unsatisfactory): "Initiative in serious jeopardy. Unlikely to realize objectives absent significant management intervention" (U.S. Government 2006).

Another set of government performance metrics has been developed by Robert S. Kaplan and David P. Norton; it is called the "balanced scorecard." In an Office of Personnel management newsletter Kaplan and Norton compare the balanced scorecard "to the dials and indicators in an airplane cockpit. For the complex task of flying an airplane, pilots need detailed information about fuel, air speed, altitude, bearing, and other indicators that summarize the current and predicted environment. Reliance on one instrument can be fatal. Similarly, the complexity of managing an organization requires that managers be able to view performance in several areas simultaneously. A balanced scorecard or a balanced set of measures provides that valuable information." (OPM 1996) In order to generate a balanced scorecard, information is gathered from four perspectives: (1) the customer's perspective, (2) the internal business perspective, (3) the innovation and learning perspective, and (4) the financial perspective. (OPM 1996) This is an important lesson to learn for generating metrics across the board: A variety of perspectives should be used so that all metrics are balanced and thus, in Clark's framework "credible."

However, of course, public performance metrics will be quite different from private performance metrics. In *Translating Performance Metrics from the Private to the Public Sector*, Paul Arveson writes that all "governmental agencies exist not for profit but to fulfill their charter or mission, which is an 'inherently governmental function.' Hence, unlike private-sector businesses that can change in any way they please, government agencies are constrained to work within their authorized mission. On the other hand, private corporations are prohibited from engaging in some activities that are authorized for the government only; these exclusions are described in the Constitution." (Arveson 1999) Therefore, there will be many differences between metrics designed for the private sector and those designed for the public sector. Arveson writes that "The key metric for government (or nonprofit) performance, therefore, is not financial in nature, but rather mission effectiveness. But mission effectiveness is not a definite and static thing." (Arveson 1999) Arveson goes on to translate the performance metrics from the private to the public world. "For instance, competitiveness in the private world translates into mission effectiveness in the public world; profit, growth, and market share in the private world translate into cost reduction and efficiency in the public world; and innovation, creativity, and good will in the private world translate into recognition, accountability to public, integrity, and fairness in the public world." (Arveson 1999) The lesson for generating metrics in general (and for generating HR metrics more specifically) is that before you generate performance metrics you must know what the purpose of the firm is (and this is a special case of Clark's "relevancy" condition) and whether it is a private firm that must respond to market conditions or a public agency that has to respond to the will of the people, regulations, and its governmentally defined mission.

Certifications as Benchmarks

Some industries use benchmarks, where if a person has some X, say a certification, then you can say that a person can achieve a certain level of performance. This is true of computer programmers who, once they possess certain certifications, are considered to possess certain skills, and thus they are competent to have certain jobs and to perform the tasks associated with those jobs. Recent years have seen a rise in demand for IT security certifications and an increase in the number of certifications being offered. This rise in demand has also been accompanied by a shift in the type of certifications available. Certifications were originally developed to sell professional services and were offered by vendors or resellers and thus driven by vendor interests. The job market is clearly the major driver behind certifications. Individuals seeking employment find it easier to get a job in the information security field if they hold a certification. Additionally, many employers offer pay bonuses for certificate holders. Certifications are basically Yes/No binary operators which function as metrics; either you have the certification or you do you do not. This is one of the ways that performance is measured in the IT industry.

However, it is possible that IT certifications do not measure performance and actually only measure how someone has done on a test. There are two potential routes we could take here. We could say (1) that other metrics of performance should be used in the IT industry, or (2) that the metrics used to generate and grade the tests are the metrics that would be really interesting to look at. Even if (1) is true it is possible that (2) is also true.

While there are several efforts under way to create a set of standards or best practices for IT security, no single consensus in this area has emerged. There is not, therefore, one agreed upon knowledge base around which certifications should be designed or one set of metrics to measure the competence of an IT security professional. With this lack of guidelines, each certification in the Information Security field has developed its own concept of what a security professional should know

Several specific requirements are worth mentioning as particularly relevant for IT security certifications. These include fair and equitable policies and procedures; documentation of how the certifying body is independent, impartial, and ethical in its decision making ("legitimacy" in Clark's words); a structure that allows participation of all interested parties; if training is provided, evidence that it does not compromise the certification process and "teach to the test" (ANSI 1999); evidence of a formal process accepted by stakeholders regarding competence for entry into the field; and review of examination/assessment development process by a psychometrician.

There is another set of standards aimed solely at the "professional and technical issues of test development," and test development could be thought of as little more than the development of metrics. Developed jointly by the American Educational Research Association, the American Psychological Association, and the National Council on Measurement in Education, these are called the Standards for Educational and Psychological Testing. (APA 1999) They address how a test is constructed, evaluated, and documented, plus fairness in testing procedures and testing applications. These standards are incredibly detailed and technical, suggesting that the most practical course of action for many certification providers would be to hire a psychometrician or other professional familiar with such procedures to guide the test development process. A few of the highlighted themes in the Standards for Educational and Psychological testing include the importance of ensuring the validity of the test (that evidence and theory support the interpretations of test scores), the reliability of the test (that measurements are consistent when the test is given to many people), and the appropriateness of test statistics.

The existence of all these standards should not suggest that developing a sound methodology is simple or that there is little room for disagreement. Even in areas like the SAT (a form of measuring competency through examination, making it similar to many certifications), which has been administered to high-schoolers since 1926, questions are still raised. Despite the test's longevity there is still debate over what we should look for in college applicants, whether the SAT measures any of those metrics at all, and whether it is biased. Many colleges and universities are even starting to make the SAT optional for applicants. All of this is to say that developing sound certification processes is difficult and not without debate, but this does not take away from the fact that best practices should be attempted and discussed. What this discussion of certification shows more generally for the discussion of metrics is that you have to make sure that you're measuring performance and not the potential ability to do something. In addition, the discussion of how certification tests are generated gives us some insight into how metrics in general should be generated. They should be developed by external bodies using legitimate practices that the players buy in to.

Teachers. One thing that many people agree on is that the state of our nation's schools is in trouble. Teacher evaluation and metrics is one of the most contentious areas where metrics are being used. It is incredibly difficult to measure the performance of teachers and it is also a political battleground, which makes the process even messier. However, generating these metrics can potentially aid the cause of educating our youth. Dan Condron, in testimony before the Subcommittee on Postsecondary Education, Training and Life-Long Learning, said, "We should provide incentive funding for states and districts to develop and implement value added or other systems for evaluating teachers based on student performance and who use their metrics to increase the skills of the existing teacher base." (Condron 2000)

The question is how can we come to an agreement as to what the performance of a school should be and how it should be measured? The most high profile area in education where metrics have been used is in the No Child Left Behind Act (2001), which is part of what is known as the accountability movement. It "puts a priority on teacher quality, as determined primarily by the evaluation process. But in evaluating teachers for purposes of accountability, principals face the public's perception that it is almost impossible to terminate a teacher for incompetent instruction. This perception is reinforced by professional literature which gives the impression that the courts place heavy demands on districts in cases involving teacher evaluation." (Zirkel 2004) The No Child Left

Behind Act (NCLBA) focuses on metrics used to measure the performance of schools. To this end "states must develop and implement a single, statewide accountability system that will be effective in ensuring that all districts and schools make adequate yearly progress, and hold accountable those that do not. States must specify annual objectives to measure progress of schools and districts to ensure that all groups of students—including low-income students, students from major racial and ethnic groups, students with disabilities, and students with limited English proficiency—reach proficiency within 12 years. States must set intermediate goals that provide for adequate yearly progress targets, with the first increase to occur no later than 2004–2005. In order to make adequate yearly progress, schools must test at least 95 percent of their students in each of the above groups." (U.S. Government 2001) The accountability movement might have wanted only to focus its aim at the school level, but once schools were supposed to be held accountable then performance metrics for teachers were inevitable. Another result of the NCLBA is that a market has sprung up for performance metrics services for schools.

One company that provides a solution to the teacher performance metrics is SPSS. SPSS Performance Metrics Jumpstart claims to be able to help "you learn how to develop a measurement system that delivers accurate performance data on your programs, services, and courses." (SPSS 2006) It does this by providing users the skills to: "Justify and maximize your budget appropriation using reliable performance data, measure participant satisfaction with programs and services via a survey design system, monitor program effectiveness by establishing key performance indicators (KPIs) and key performance predictors (KPPs), maximize program and service delivery by deploying KPI and KPP models throughout your organization, isolate predictors of superior service delivery through analysis of data stores, and react quickly to performance problems via an early warning system." (SPSS 2006) Such products and companies provide a great service in terms of teacher performance metrics.

However, the main problem with teacher performance metrics is that people (experts included) can't seem to agree on what these metrics should measure. Therefore, the products that are being marketed now might be used across a school district (which is a fairly high level of standardization) or they might just be used in one school (which is a fairly low level of standardization). As a result of the lack of standardization in teacher performance metrics a teacher that scores well on one performance metric might not perform well on another. This leads to confusion (and perhaps arises out of a more basic confusion, which is that we don't agree on what the performance of a good teacher is supposed to look like).

What this means for the generation of HR performance metrics is that it is in our interest to come up with industry-wide standards for HR performance metrics, for only then we will truly be able to reap the benefits of such metrics. In order to generate such standardized metrics, we have to agree on what performance in human resources means. This task requires a great deal of introspection and discussion.

One nonprofit organization that helps standardize a variety of metrics is the American National Standards Institute (ANSI) which "coordinates the development and use of voluntary consensus standards in the United States and represents the needs and views of U.S. stakeholders in standardization forums around the globe." (ANSI 2006) Use of such an organization or the development of a new organization that helped industries standardize their metrics would be extremely helpful for the development of performance metrics.

Further, people can't agree on what to do with performance metrics once they are generated. The main question here is whether they should be used to determine teacher's pay. At issue is what is known in the education world as Performance Pay. The way teacher pay primarily works is that teachers climb step by lockstep up a traditional pay ladder, which entails automatically earning salary increases based on their education level and their years of service without reference to their performance on the job. However, "the trend toward performance-based pay for educators is a growing one." (Rotherham 2000) Already "30 out of 50 states passed legislation requiring some type of performance pay for teachers, or some portion of teacher pay," Dr. Marc J. Wallace Jr., founding partner of the Center for Workforce Effectiveness, is quoted as saying. (Delisio 2003)

People in favor of performance pay claim that implementing such schemes "will attract more people to the teaching profession and make those in the profession work harder." (Delisio 2003) On the other side of the fence are those who argue that "any type of system tying salaries to teacher performance or student outcomes is flawed because of a lack of objective observers and objective criteria to evaluate a teacher's performance." (Delisio 2003) However, those on this latter side of the fence are perhaps merely saying that adequate performance metrics have not been generated. But such standards could possibly be generated if people came together to create metrics that were "credible," "relevant," and "legitimate." And indeed, this is one of the mistakes that people make about metrics, that they must be objective to be worthwhile. In fact, very few people will ever believe any performance metric is objective. What we need are metrics that are "credible," "relevant," and "legitimate." Metrics meeting those criteria can only be generated if experts and practitioners in the industry at hand can come together to discuss what performance in that industry is supposed to mean. This lesson is no less true for human resources than it is for education.

In addition, those who are opposed to performance pay note the possibility that such measures of output could be manipulated. (Rothstein 2000) This points to yet another lesson for those generating performance metrics. These data outputs in these performance metrics should be subject to high data protection standards, not merely so that those metrics will not be manipulated (although this should be reason enough) but also so that the firms generating such metrics are not held civilly or criminally liable for security breaches that allow the data collected to be compromised. Such data protection regimes should be instituted before performance metrics are put in place.

Crime. Metrics are, of course, necessary not only for the good, but also for darker elements as well. Crime is one area where metrics are needed, but also where they are strangely difficult to come by. How do we measure the performance of law enforcement in various communities? One of the ways we do this is via crime statistics. Crime statistics are compiled by two major sources for overall national crime statistics, the Uniform Crime Reports (UCR) and the National Crime Victimization Survey (NCVS).

The UCR began in 1929 following an initiative of the International Association of Chiefs of Police (IACP). The UCR is a measure only of crime that is reported to the police. As reporting in the UCR Program is voluntarily done by law enforcement agencies, the UCR lacks standardization across jurisdictions. Standardization is one problem that runs through any study of metrics. One fix to this problem is to have an external body manage the metrics for an entire industry.

The problem with the lack of standardization in crime statistics means that certain crimes are classified in different ways in different communities, therefore altering the crime statistics for that community and how the public views the performance of law enforcement officers. It should be noted that changing these crime statistics can have immense political consequences (and can be equally instigated by political motivations). For instance, charges of manipulation of crime statistics have been brought in New York City, Atlanta, Boca Raton, and Philadelphia, resulting in several resignations and dismissals as evidence of political tampering of numbers was uncovered in these cities. (Butterfield 1998) These cases are just a reminder that performance metrics can come under immense political pressure. Such pressure to change the data can come from governmental agencies, from the management within a firm, or from outside the company. If the pressure is given in to, the performance metrics used become meaningless.

The NCVS is a national survey of 42,000 households regarding incidents of victimization. Since it is a survey of the population, the NCVS provides an account of crime whether or not it has been reported to the police. So while it should provide a count similar to the UCR, it is somewhat different due to the fact that the UCR is reported by police and the NCVS is reported by citizens. The difficulty with the NCVS is that some respondents may not remember particular incidents or specific details of crimes, or they may conflate two crimes, or they may "remember" crimes that have happened to other people. The lesson for performance metrics here is that we should not forget that people's psychology plays a role in how they answer questions, which might be a part of performance metrics. This is perhaps particularly true in human resources, where individuals might be answering questions about colleagues about whom they have complex feelings.

Ten Lessons from the Field

All of the metrics explored have taught us important lessons about performance metrics.

1. Metrics should be "credible," "relevant," and "legitimate."
2. Metrics should actually measure the thing that you want them to.
3. Performance metrics should be external metrics, not internal ones.
4. Before you generate performance metrics you must know what the purpose of the firm is (and whether it is public or private).
5. Performance metrics that are benchmarks might not actually measure performance.

6. The results of performance metrics might be counter intuitive, so it will take a lot to get people (especially managers) on board.

7. There should be industry-wide standards for the generation of performance metrics (perhaps an organization should be started to help industries establish performance metrics standards).

8. Performance metrics can come under immense political pressure.

9. High data protection standards should be used to ensure the integrity of the performance metrics at hand.

10. Finally, we should not forget that people's psychology plays a role in how they answer questions that might be a part of performance metrics.

If all of the these lessons are adhered to, human resources performance metrics will mean a lot more and will have the potential to help the industry a lot more, since metrics serve as a foundation for running a successful business.

CHAPTER

12

Case Studies—Metrics in Action

The metrics discussed in Chapters 8 and 9 have successfully been implemented and utilized by many types of organizations, helping them to improve staffing operations to assist in the attainment of strategic business goals. Survey research by Staffing.org indicates, for example, that a vast majority of organizations have reported that setting agreed upon start dates for new hires has significantly improved the percentage of new employees starting on time. One such organization is PacifiCare Health Systems, where the utilization of such metrics has helped the organization accomplish its goal of changing its culture.

Sherri Bliss: Program Manager, PacifiCare Health Systems

Please describe your recruiting metrics program and how it is used. (metrics for management reporting, metrics for Human Resources reporting, and recruiter productivity metrics).

As one of the nation's leading consumer health organizations,

PacifiCare is recognized for innovation in consumer products and services, as well as our employment practices. In business for more than 26 years, we employ approximately 9,100 employees and do business in 36 states and Guam.

Launched in January 2002 as part of a business turnaround strategy, PacifiCare's Talent Acquisition department is responsible for the acquisition of human capital through strategic recruitment and branding programs to meet the business challenges and objectives of PacifiCare and assure we are hiring for fit in an achievement culture. Committed to the employment brand we created, "Envision. Innovate. Accomplish," our department was integral to the success of a business turnaround strategy launched in 2000, officially accomplished at the end of 2004, by facilitating the company's shift to an achievement culture through talent acquisition and development. Over our 3+ years in operation, we have grown into a world class recruiting organization with notable accomplishments.

In order to evaluate our effectiveness and opportunities for improvement as a staffing function, we have been measuring and reporting a specific set of metrics since our inception. Our key performance metrics at present include Staffing Efficiency Ratio, Hiring Manager Satisfaction, Timely Requisition Fulfillment via a Time Ratio, Employee Referral Hires, Employee Ethnicity Trend and Underutilized Position Fulfillment. We historically measured Quality of Hire via Employee Turnover and Retention statistics, but continue to search for better ways to measure and evaluate new hire quality.

These metrics are used both to evaluate individual and team performance within the department, as well as to report performance to our Office of the President, made up of the senior-most business leaders from throughout PacifiCare's operations. In addition, metrics are used to evaluate business trends, root cause analysis, and assist in strategic planning on a quarterly and annual basis.

What was the reasoning and strategy behind your metrics program and how has it developed?

Our metrics program has evolved to align with expert recommendations and business need. We align our metrics to what matters to the business to assure we are always concentrating on the right measures. For example, our Employee Ethnicity Trend and Underutilized Fulfillment Rate are unique and particularly relevant metrics for PacifiCare's strategic diversity vision. We measure the ethnic and gender diversity of our employees quarterly to determine if our diversity recruitment and affirmative action plans are resulting in PacifiCare's workforce demographics becoming more reflective of our diverse membership and the communities we serve. We have been successful in changing the ethnicity trends over the past two years, increasing the non-white exempt population by 11.81 percent, which we believe will make a positive impact on our membership and revenue as well.

In addition to the aforementioned metrics, we gather data to determine how the recruitment experience impacts PacifiCare's brand among candidates who are interviewed in person for a position with PacifiCare, as well as how the onboarding experience impacts retention and turnover. In January 2004, PacifiCare's Recruitment Department implemented an on-line interview experience survey for all candidates who are in-person interviewed for a position with PacifiCare, whether or not the person is given a job offer, and whether or not the person accepts or declines the offer in cases where an offer is given. We also implemented retention and turnover surveys so that employees who terminate voluntarily from the company within six months of their start date are surveyed about onboarding and other issues that may have impacted the quick turnover, while employees who reach their six-month anniversary with PacifiCare receive a similar survey to gauge retention inputs. The e-mail based survey instrument was designed in conjunction with Genesee Survey Services, a recognized leader in the field of employee surveys. Not only is the use of an on-line, e-mail based survey tool an innovative utilization of survey technology to enhance our metrics process and breadth, but it also demonstrates our commitment to innovative metrics that have a large-scale impact on PacifiCare's overall employment brand.

What metrics did you decide not to include in your program and why?

Although some benchmark reports still measure cost per hire, that has not been a metric we have used in our history at PacifiCare. Because we were implementing a new in-house centralized recruitment model at the time of our department launch, our comparative metric to evaluate performance around cost was the annual amount spent on external staffing firms. Hiring Managers at PacifiCare, while there was no dedicated recruitment department, had become reliant on placement agencies and had budgeted accordingly for agency fees. The Recruiting Efficiency Ratio, the metric we selected to use to measure our cost efficiency, served as a better method of comparison between the former model and the new. The Recruiting Efficiency Ratio, which we learned about from Staffing.org, is the calculation of the total recruitment expenses of an organization divided by the total salaries recruited in a given period.

We also have stopped measuring Time-to-Fill and Time-to-Start for requisition fulfillment. Based on the benchmark report from Staffing.org, the most important metric regarding recruitment time is that the new hire has effectively started work per a mutually agreed upon "contracted start date" between the Hiring Manager and the Recruiter. Staffing.org suggests the Time Metric or the ratio of the Actual Time-to-Start divided by the Contracted Time-to-Start. The actual time is the number of days between when recruiting is initiated and when the new employee starts. The contracted time is the number of days between the date recruiting is initiated and the date the recruiter and hiring manager mutually agree that the position will be filled. PacifiCare was able to implement a customized data field within our requisition process with

VirtualEdge, our Enterprise Staffing Software provider, that captures the "contracted start date" and to create a customized report to calculate Time for each requisition and for all requisitions filled within a given period of time. We have been using that report to track the Time Metric since Q3 2004.

How are outcomes translated into action in your organization?

As mentioned previously, our metrics are used to develop annual goals for continuous improvement.

What's great about your program? What remains a challenge?

The two things I am most proud of our metrics program accomplishing are:

1. Our ability to quantitatively measure our performance year over year and in comparison to external benchmarks is something that I am very proud of. The program allows us to determine if we have been successful or seen improvement in the high priority areas for our company through objective, validated measures. Our metrics program has enabled us to effectively support PacifiCare's corporate brand and our own employment brand through external recognition.

Our department has consistently performed better than the industry and all-company benchmark in Efficiency, Hiring Manager Satisfaction and Time Metrics when compared with the Staffing.org annual benchmarking survey. We believe our performance has been outstanding for many reasons, among which is the fact that we do measure what is important to the business and then plan accordingly so that we can excel in our performance.

2. Another source of pride comes from our focus on diversity and affirmative action metrics, which has also reaped tremendous recognition for PacifiCare as an employer of choice. In 2004 and 2005, PacifiCare was recognized as a Fortune Top 50 Employer for Minorities and Top 50 Employer for Women in 2005, Top 10 Employer for Asian Americans by Asian Enterprise Magazine (2004 and 2005), a Hispanic 100 Employer of Choice by Hispanic Magazine (2004 and 2005), a Top Company for Latinas by Latina Style Magazine (2004 and 2005), a Top Company for Minorities by Hispanic Business magazine and Company of the Year by the Black Chamber of Commerce of Orange County.

This year we also won the Electronic Recruiting Exchange award for Most Effective Use of Staffing Metrics, the Power to Perform Award from VirtualEdge and were a finalist for the American Business Awards in the Outstanding Human Resources Team category.

Our biggest challenge remains effectively measuring the quality of hire of our new hires. In addition, there is significant room for improvement around integration of our various reporting systems for a simplified data collection, reporting and analysis process.

What is your frequency of outcomes reporting and of data collection?

Individual recruiter metrics, which include hiring manager satisfaction and the time ratio, are reported to our staffing director monthly. Our other metrics are aggregated to the department level and reported to PacifiCare's Executive Management team quarterly within the Human Resources Quarterly Business Review. Based on each quarter's metrics and annualized trends, priority areas for improvement or growth are identified and prioritized.

How much data is collected manually and how much is collected automatically?

Our metrics are managed by gathering relevant information through various support systems including our HRIS, PeopleSoft, our applicant tracking system, VirtualEdge, our financial system, Oracle, and our survey tool, Insight Express. All necessary reporting fields in each system have been captured in customized reports, and are available within our reporting portals for each system. The ease-of-use of these reports with pre-designated reporting criteria enables any member of the recruitment department to capture metrics information anytime. We have also worked with VirtualEdge to customize the system to accommodate our metrics process. For example, in early 2005, VirtualEdge added a field to our requisition database for "contracted start date" and created a custom report to track our Time Ratio, the time metric most highly valued by Hiring Managers according to Staffing.org.

Our Hiring Manager Satisfaction Survey is administered through Insight Express's award-winning technology that allows for more sophisticated data analysis of survey data.

Once all data is collected, the process of calculating specific metrics is a manual process performed within Excel. A template workbook was designed in 2002, our first year of reporting data, and the process is now more a series of data entry activities, with follow-up trend analysis. The data from Excel is later input into a dashboard format for the recruitment team and into a PowerPoint presentation for senior management. The entire metrics process each quarter takes approximately four hours in total.

Do you have a data collection tip you can share with others?

Own and integrate as many of the reporting or tracking tools as possible for easy access.

Have you ever used metrics to build a business case?

· In the fall of 2004, a business case was made around our process and cost efficiencies to support the centralization of our nonexempt recruitment function. Our Exempt Staffing Cost Ratio showed a significant reduction in exempt hiring costs throughout 2003 and 2004 following centralization of exempt recruiting. Based on these results, we centralized all nonexempt hiring beginning January, 2005. Senior management approved the business case, and the centralization was implemented in January, 2005. Based on Q1 and Q2 results for 2005 that centralization of all recruiting has continued to drive down our staffing costs.

In early 2005, our Employee Ethnicity Trend and tracking of Ethnic Diversity Hiring enabled us to make the business case for further alignment with our full suite of Consumer Initiatives targeting ethnic minorities and women. In prior years, with our Latino Health Solutions Division, we developed and maintained important partnerships with Latino organizations that enabled us to increase the number of Latino hires at all levels of the organization. Through our metrics reporting, we noticed that this trend did not exist within African American and Asian American demographics. We took that as a sign that our diversity efforts needed expansion into additional ethnic and gender groups. We have since begun to implement a similar partnering process with our African American Health Solutions and Asian American Markets groups.

We also plan to use the data around our aforementioned retention and turnover surveys to build a business case for a more comprehensive onboarding program.

Do you use any internal or external benchmarks?

We continually compare our quarter to quarter and annualized performance to identify trends, areas in need of improvement, and areas where we have excelled over time. In addition, we use the Staffing.org annual Recruiting Metrics and Performance Benchmark Report to determine how we are performing in comparison to other companies both within the health care industry and in other industries.

Do you assess correlations in your data?

Any correlation analysis we conduct is on an ad hoc basis and is conducted manually.

Metrics Help Intel Leap Ahead

Another organization that has significantly benefited from the application and implementation of metrics is the Intel Corporation.

The following section describes the ways in which Intel has used metrics as well as its expectations of those metrics and associated programs.

Intel Corporation's Global Staffing (GS) works to attract and hire talent in over 50 countries to fuel Intel's platform and technology advancement that become essential to the way we work and live. In 2005, Intel Global Staffing launched a three-year program called Staffing Success Strategy (S^3) to support Intel's future needs and to become world-class in all of its operations. See Figure 12.1, Global Staffing End State: World Class Organization by 2007.

Intel's Staffing Success Strategic Objectives

- Deliver cutting-edge workforce planning solutions.
- Build the world's strongest sourcing capabilities.
- Deliver world-class hiring services.
- Operate with excellence.

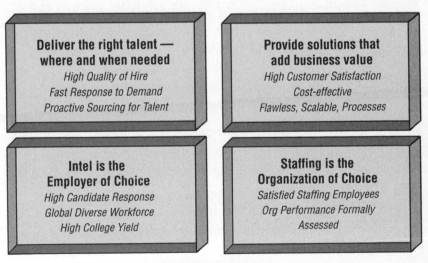

Figure 12.1

Global Staffing has specific deliverables aligned with each of these strategic objectives with measurements associated with each deliverable. The three-year roadmap is reviewed for progress against schedule.

Intel's metrics portfolio is a key resource to guide the management of this staffing effort and in the attainment of world-class performance. The suite of metrics was recently re-engineered to support S^3, and to align with the overall Human Resources (HR) business objectives.

The re-engineered metric portfolio allowed management to see business conditions in new ways in 2005, a year when Intel added 20,000 new employees. Intel has had a staffing metrics portfolio for some time. The refreshed portfolio leverages the earnings from that first effort. The new portfolio is a prominent management tool to guide the application of resources to manage the essentials of the staffing function. See Table 12.1.

INTRODUCTION TO INTEL'S STAFFING METRICS PORTFOLIO

New Hire Quality. The New Hire Quality metric was adapted from a Recruiting Roundtable white paper (Recruiting Roundtable 2004)..(See Figure 12.2 and Table 12.2.)

This assessment of Intel's new employees is obtained from the hiring manager and from the new employee. Survey responses are supplemented with organizational and other data to increase the value of analysis. Quality of Hire summary data provides insight into which organizations routinely do well as well as those where improvement is needed. This data provides the basis for a management conversation.

Speed of Hire. Intel's "need for speed" is great, not only for product performance, but recruiting talent at the right time. Global Staffing implemented the Time-to-Target metric (also known as

Table 12.1

Metric Name	Category	Measures	Frequency
Quality of Hire	Quality	Analysis of three dimensions: Manager's and new employee's assessment of job-fit, organization-fit, and effective integration.	Monthly
Recruiting Cost Ratio	Cost	Total Recruiting Costs divided by Total Compensation Recruited; measures staffing costs across the multi-national environment.	Quarterly
Actual/Contracted Time to Start (Time-to-Target)	Time	Measures the difference between actual and projected (target) start date for external offers. Measures if new talent is delivered when the business needs it.	Monthly
Key Stakeholder Interview	Satisfaction	Senior business manager assessment of the relationship with Global Staffing.	Semi-annually
Hiring Manager Satisfaction	Satisfaction	Measures satisfaction of hiring manager with services, tools, and candidate quality.	Monthly
Proactive Sourcing	Sourcing	Measures percentage of candidates who receive offers and who have resumes in Resume database before the requisition was opened; measures if the talent pipeline is filled in anticipation of future demand.	Monthly

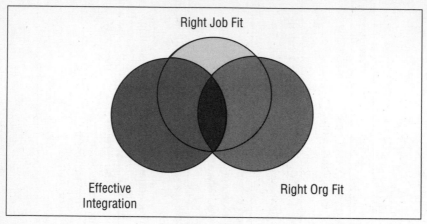

Figure 12.2

Table 12.2

Dimension	Attribute
Job Fit	Necessary skills
Organization Fit	Culture/values alignment
Integration	Process effectiveness

Contacted/Actual Time to Start) to ensure the speed of hire expectations are met. See Figure 12.3.

This measure is based on the expectation that Staffing will take seriously an agreed-upon date (negotiated with the hiring manager, if necessary) when the requisition will be filled.

Time-to-Target Aid: Projected Start Date Tool. This tool provides GS Staff with historical Time-to-Start requisition data (country, job, class, job grade, etc.). Using this information, GS can manage and negotiate expectations with hiring managers.

Hiring Manager Satisfaction. Intel measures satisfaction with the staffing organization at two levels: hiring managers and senior managers. Hiring manager satisfaction plays a prominent tactical role in assessing satisfaction with (a) services provided by the

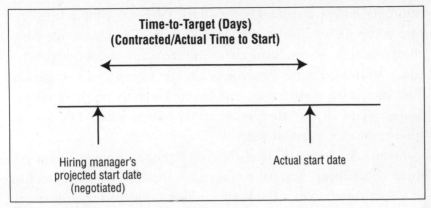

Figure 12.3

Staffing Consultant throughout the hiring process; (b) quality of candidates received; (c) hiring tools; and (d) overall experience as a hiring manager. Each month's results are studied for trends and the detailed verbatim responses. Senior manager satisfaction is assessed by the "Key Stakeholder Interview," which measures satisfaction with the business relationship with staffing.

Staffing Cost and Efficiency. Intel faces the challenge of measuring staffing efficiency in more than 50 countries. The legacy metric "Cost per Hire" is not useful for Intel due to the wide variation in the economies of the numerous countries Intel is engaged in and the wide range of associated skill sets.

Intel introduced the new metrics, Recruiting Cost Ratio, to measure its staffing costs, and Recruiting Efficiency to measure efficiency and compare itself with other organizations. These metrics compute the ratio of Total Recruiting Costs to Total Compensation Recruited. They provide clear visibility of our recruiting costs and efficiency across all Intel organizations. Because these metrics express recruiting costs against compensation recruited, Intel believes these measures are comparable across the 50-plus countries in which we recruit.

Proactive Sourcing. Intel has a keen interest in identifying targeted talent in anticipation of future staffing demands. Its "Proactive

Sourcing" metric measures how well the talent pipeline is filled before a specific requisition becomes known. This metric measures the percentage of candidates who receive offers and who have resumes in Intel's resume database before the requisition was opened. This metric has a synergistic and beneficial effect on the Time-to-Target metric. If the talent is already known to Intel, then we can fill a requisition expeditiously.

Metrics Are Improving Intel's Staffing Processes. Regional management conducts operational reviews each month with the Directors of Global Staffing in attendance. Trends are judged against established targets. The discussions are focused on operational metric improvement.

A specific example of how Intel's metrics have worked together to improve our staffing process is evident in the performance of the European Staffing Group. In the first half of 2005, Intel base lined performance to its metrics. Evaluation of the base-line data revealed that the European region was performing well below the goals in many of their key metrics. Once focused effort was given to improvement, the European region saw steady improvement in all established measures. Proactively sourced candidates increased while cost for recruitment steadily decreased. Another result of more effective proactive sourcing in this region was the ability to better meet the business needs for headcount resources. Improvement in this area was reflected in improved performance around Time-to-Target. Lastly, a steady improvement in overall customer satisfaction was evident. Intel's re-engineered metrics are driving improvement in the processes and this improvement is directly tied to Intel's effectiveness as an organization and overall customer satisfaction.

Metrics Are Helping Intel Acquire Better People. New Intel employees add to the strength of a corporation which is consistently profitable and innovative in the delivery of new platforms and technology. To drive developments of complete technology platforms, Intel has organized all major product groups around five business platforms: mobility, digital enterprise, digital home, digital healthcare, and channel platforms. New employees with skill sets not traditionally hired by the Intel Corporation are driving product delivery within these new platform organizations.

As noted above, Quality of Hire at Intel is based on an assessment of three dimensions: job fit, organization fit, and effective integration. In conversations with the Recruiting Roundtable, Intel has learned that their results for New Hire Quality, when benchmarked against the collected data available from Recruiting Roundtable, are substantially more favorable. In addition, they have found a very high congruence between the assessments made by the hiring managers and the new employees; both populations summarize the same conclusions. Analysis of New Hire Quality results can be focused at the business group level where detailed results reveal strengths and areas for improvement.

Staffing Metrics Align with Human Resources General Metrics. Intel's staffing metric portfolio paints an accurate picture of the condition of the staffing function. Findings are presented quarterly to senior Human Resources executives. This management review may lead to new conversations about where to put emphasis of effort for the benefit of Intel's stakeholders.

Human Resources professionals outside of staffing are asked to support the metric portfolio by communicating key messages, especially concerning New Hire Quality and Time-to-Target, to their business counterparts. The necessity of frequent and focused communication about the staffing metrics portfolio to the rest of Human Resources is especially relevant since Intel's most strategic measures are innovative and as a result require a new way of thinking about the practical implications of the execution of the metric portfolio.

Business needs drive the use of innovative data-gathering technologies.

Efficient delivery of Intel's metrics requires use of appropriate technology: See Table 12.3.

Table 12.3

Deliverable	Appropriate Technology
Recruiting Efficiency Ratio	Database extract
Quality of Hire	Intranet web process using non-procedural survey software
Actual/Contracted Time to Start (Time-to-Target)	Database extract
Key Stakeholder Interview	Intranet web process using non-procedural survey software
Proactive Sourcing	Database extract
Metrics Dashboard (a more advanced Dashboard will be delivered in 2006)	Intranet web process with results displayed with nonprocedural presentation software
Detailed Metric Data	Metric outcomes are also presented in spreadsheet or PC-based database format which allows for detailed analysis, if warranted.
Metrics Library (repository of tutorial and reference material)	Intranet web process

Metrics Boost Intel's Competitive Advantage. The depth and breadth of capacity in Intel to deliver advanced technology in its five major platform organizations is directly attributable to the success in attracting, selecting, hiring and retaining high performance talent. Intel's metrics portfolio is fundamental to this strategic requirement.

Intel believes its current portfolio measures the essential performance areas for its staffing organization. The management attention given to the metric information has a direct and observable benefit that Intel's stakeholders can see in their terms. They have also shown that metric improvement leads to improved business performance in areas meaningful to stakeholders: the quality of hires, delivery of talent when needed by the business, proactive identification of talent, and efficient use of Intel's assets. Where improvement is needed, the metric portfolio tells them where they need to focus.

The direct connection between the work performed by Intel's Staffing organization and Intel's ability to remain competitive and on the leading edge of innovation has been clearly shown. There is a strong correlation between delivery of Intel's metrics information and a quality hire delivered when the business needs it. The portfolio makes evident both Intel's strengths and where further improvement is needed. The metrics program gives a practical outlet to focus the Intel energy for continuous improvement.

Human Capital and Organizational Performance

Leading-Lagging Indicator Relationships

Businesses measure processes and outcomes as a gauge of performance. Gross Sales, Costs of Goods, Inventory, and Expenses are common examples. These are often called lagging indicators, as they measure the results of people's efforts. In contrast, individual behaviors can be considered leading indicators, because they contribute to or produce the results.

In retail terms, the marketing department may argue that store traffic might be a leading indicator connected to the lagging indicator of sales. The training department may assert that the lagging indicator of sales is driven by the leading indicator of the percentage of employees completing a sales training course. The recruiting team may insist that better talent at the time of hire is the leading indicator driving sales. The individual attributes (that were screened for at the time of hire) can be considered leading indicators, those which contribute to or produce the desired behaviors.

In reality, these are all variables in the value creation chain. In the above examples, the leading indicator for one measure may be the lagging indicator of another. The better the understanding of the leading-lagging relationships, the better prepared an organization is for taking actions that can impact business results.

There are three sets of measurable components regarding human factors:

1. Attributes.
2. Behaviors.
3. Results.

The relationship between these three variables is presented in Figure 13.1 in a two-tier model for leading-lagging indicator relationships. The model is as follows:

• Staffing Relationships—Attributes to Behaviors.
• Management Relationships—Behaviors to Results.

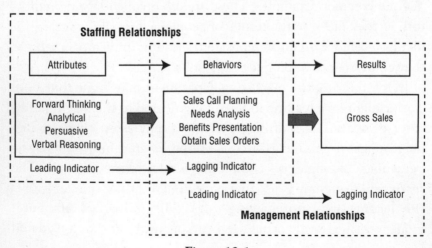

Figure 13.1

Attributes or human factors are referred to as underlying traits, characteristics, and capabilities. Attributes can be organized into a range of categories, such as:

- Sensory—Sight, hearing, touch, smell, taste.
- Physical—Capabilities to lift, push, pull, climb, twist.
- Cognitive—Reading, math, analysis, mechanical comprehension, reasoning.
- Work style—Confidence, out-going, conceptual, conscientious, optimistic.

There are hundreds of discrete human attributes that can be measured with standardized forms of assessments. A test that measures the ability to perform addition calculations with whole numbers is one example. Behaviors are describable, observable, measurable actions of a person. Behaviors are commonly organized into categories as well:

- Working with people—Speak, listen, direct, inquire.
- Working with things—List, calculate, move, adjust, start, stop.
- Working individually—Initiate, complete.

Thousands of observable behaviors are called for in everyday work. Given a chance to compare and contrast, behaviors may be organized into ranges of effectiveness or proficiency, and ranked in terms of importance to job performance. Behavior rating scales can be created that provide a range of effectiveness or frequency of occurrence. This creates a standardized method for rating on-the-job behaviors.

Attributes and behaviors for a job or position are best identified through the process of Job Modeling. There are many approaches to accomplish this. A multi-method approach produces the most meaningful and useful results. This includes: job observation, review of existing job documentation and training materials, competency card sorts, structured questionnaires to define tasks, identification of position-specific and organizational variables as well as repertory grid analysis and documentation of work-related trends affecting those in the position.

Results are the final product or outcome of effort. Desired results vary from job to job and company to company. Organizations have invested significant resources in designing, building, and installing measurement systems to report on these lagging indicators. The output of these systems often drives decision making and action planning. Examples of results measures may include:

- Sales, over any unit of time, such as annual sales or sales orders per day.
- Parts completed per shift.
- Shrinkage (unexplained losses).
- Complaints resolved on first contact.
- Files retrieved per shift.
- Scrap rate as a percentage of materials purchased.
- Worker's compensation claims.
- Reduced accounts receivable days outstanding.

To make the two-tier relationship connection, consider a sales manager faced with a goal to expand market share. She may want salespeople who can increase market penetration and increase the value of the average transaction.

For staffing, a leading-lagging indicator relationship might be: What skills and traits or attributes are linked to create effective sales behaviors? For sales management, a leading-lagging indicator relationship might be: What behaviors are linked to creating sales?

Once the job demands for attributes and behaviors have been defined, a sound measurement system can provide the data to explore and determine what relationships exist between these variables and the achievement of business results. When a company knows how to evaluate and select candidates with attributes that have a strong link or relationship to the attainment of job objectives, they create a competitive advantage. The hiring process has moved from trial and error to trial and success.

The Matrix of Relationships

A matrix provides a strong visual display of variables and relationships. Figures 13.2 and 13.3 demonstrate a method for organizing

Does this employee:					
	Rarely	*Sometimes*	*Usually*	*Always*	*Comments*
Positive Behaviors					
Break problems into logical steps?					Positive and negative behavioral examples are captured from focus group's output.
Involve appropriate people in the problem solving process?					
Obtain all pertinent information before making decisions?					
	Rarely	*Sometimes*	*Usually*	*Always*	*Comments*
Negative Behaviors					
Jump to conclusions too soon?					
Often have to come back and rework problems a second time?					
Focus on potential solutions without adequately understanding the problem?					

Figure 13.2

1	2	3	4	5	6	7	An overall rating for each competency is made. Additionally, overall ratings of performance, promotability, and other outcomes are typically attained.
Least effective	Well below average (bottom 20%)	Below average (21–40%)	Average (41–60%)	Above average (61–79%)	Well above average (top 20%)	Most effective	

Supporting Observations

Space is provided for additional comments to support ratings.

Figure 13.3

and presenting variables to be considered for measurement in a staffing process. Figure 13.2 connects Attributes to Behaviors while Figure 13.3 connects Behaviors to Results. Once sound measures for each of the indicators are obtained, an analysis can be conducted to determine where the leading-lagging relationships exist and define the strength of the relationship. The Attribute to Behavior Matrix is shown in Table 13.1.

The Behavior to Results Matrix is shown in Table 13.2.

In 2001, a study of a data entry position was conducted for a leading regional financial services firm. It was discovered that a test (leading indicator)—one that measured the ability to accurately match a string of characters to another string found in a group of four—had a strong relationship to the volume of data fields entered per hour (lagging indicator). More data fields per hour translate into fewer people for the same volume of work, or greater volume with the same head count. Either approach provides a competitive advantage on the cost/time of throughput for data entry (lagging indicator).

Table 13.1

Attributes	Licensing Exam	Reference Checks	Communications	Job Knowledge	Supervisor Ratings	Teamwork
Cognitive Ability						
Problem Solving Test						
Math Test						
Grammar Test						
Job Simulation						
Simulated Customer Calls						
Workstyle Scales						
Tolerance for Ambiguity						
Boredom Proneness						
Coping with Pressure						
Dynamic Work Environment						
Empathy						

213

Table 13.2

	New Sales	Renewal Sales	Attendance	Customer Complaints
Licensing Exam				
Reference Checks				
Communications				
Job Knowledge				
Supervisor Ratings				
Teamwork				

In another recent study (1998 to 2002) of call center staff for a national insurance company, it was discovered that a score on problem solving assessment had a strong relationship to passing a licensing test required to perform the job. By using this data, the company reduced the number of job offers to those less likely to pass the licensing test and thus reduced training investments and associated salary costs. Oddly enough, the range in scores of those achieving well on problem solving had little to no relationship to job performance. This is an example where the leading indicator predicts a critical threshold behavior, such as passing the test, but does not have a relationship with actual job performance. The candidates need to get the license to sell, but getting the license is not an indicator of ability to sell effectively.

This type of analysis requires accurately collected, well organized data on the relevant variables. The data needed to perform analysis of this nature requires a well designed measurement system. By examining the rigor of data capture used in accounts receivable or inventory control, one can see the database structure and the frequency and scope of data entry. Applying the same level of system design, detail definition, and data entry to staffing processes can produce metrics the organization can use to support business decisions from staffing strategies.

Measures of Meaning

Individual productivity is a measure of Quality of Hire. In his book *The Deming Route to Quality and Productivity* (1988), William Scherkenbach, Ford's former Director of Statistical Methods, states: "If you believe in the Law of Averages, there will always be above-average and below-average." He goes on to explain that the quest is to raise the average.

Do you know what the "average" is of the talent you obtain with each hiring decision? The wrong hire can actually take your average down a notch. Spencer and Spencer (2001) document the output advantage of people who are one standard deviation above average in their book, *Competence at Work*. In non-sales positions, the impact is 19 percent to 48 percent more output. In sales positions, the range goes from 48 percent to 120 percent more sales volume. As such, high levels of performance have a much greater impact on the bottom line than was traditionally recognized.

In Watson Wyatt's 1999 research on the Human Capital Index®, it was found that "by showing a significant improvement in recruiting new talent, companies can achieve a 10.1 percent increase in market value—the largest found among the five areas linking . . . effective human capital practices and shareholder value creation." In staffing, New Hire Quality is raised by increasing the validity of methods used to make hiring decisions. Research into the validity of various methods used in hiring decisions was conducted at the University of Michigan.

The SHRM/AON 1997 Survey of Human Resource Trends provided summary data suggesting that those firms using more sophisticated selection methods were more satisfied with the quality of their hiring outcomes. The study also presented two contrasting perspectives:

- The greatest deficiencies in candidates were work attitudes and basic skills.

- The least commonly used selection methods of the survey respondents were the approaches designed to measure basic skills and work attitudes.

Clearly, the lessons learned from research and measurement of factors that link improved organization performance to recruiting and selection suggest that it is critical to raise the bar on how hiring decisions are made.

Creating Value. Selling the value of an investment begins with the end in mind. What will the investment do for the investor? Creating a business case for building a better selection system comes from understanding the value of a performance gap. In its most simple format, the manner to define and present a performance differential is with a visual. An above-average performer sells $2 million per year and an average performer sells $1.5 million. Multiplied over 50 hires, there is a yearly opportunity to move toward $25 million in sales growth using the same head count—but with more efficient people.

This same modeling can be used to capture performance gaps along any lagging indicator: data fields per hour, parts machined, files processed, claims resolved, days absent, and so on.

What investment has your firm's human resource department made in a system that measures and explores correlations between the leading indicators of staffing and the lagging indicators of organization performance? It is this discipline that creates measures of meaning for impacting organization performance.

Look at Your Emphasis. Management authority and business author Peter F. Drucker once said, "If you can't measure what is important, what you do measure becomes important." This is a call for human resource practitioners to reflect on the value of the measures they capture and report to the organization.

In general, companies seek to reduce cost and increase value or quality. Think about the consequences here. If you report costs, you will be asked to make that number smaller. This may mean,

"Reduce your cost-per-hire." While it is a good thing to be cost effective, this may be a low payoff activity. Why? According to the 2001 EMA/SHRM Cost-per-Hire Survey, the average transaction cost was just over $2,500. If you work to obtain a 10 percent reduction, you save $250. No doubt this is real money, and worth being sensitive to. However, it may not cost more to hire a candidate who can perform at a higher level of productivity; it may even be worth spending $250 more to increase the likelihood of hiring a real winner. Spencer and Spencer's research shows that hiring a real winner is worth at least a 19 percent performance gain, which is worth far more than $250. A quick survey of any line manager can provide you with performance data that demonstrates the value of average versus above-average performers in their department. These people were most likely hired by the same method, at the same cost-per-hire. To verify this assumption, ask the hiring manager if he or she would be willing to invest a bit more in the staffing process to get more above-average performers. This gives you insight into a hiring manager's view of New Hire Quality.

If you report on the New Hire Quality, you may be asked to increase that quality. New Hire Quality is a term that implies delivering to the customer's (hiring manager) specifications. For data entry, for example, it may be more keystrokes per hour at an accuracy level of 99.7 percent. For manufacturing, this might mean shorter set-up time on milling operations. When your staffing process measures and demonstrates a sound link between candidate attributes and business outcomes, your system is measuring the quality of hire. This is the key to managing how value is created with every hiring decision. And this is the key to managing the value creation of a human capital investment.

These steps will drive better measures and stronger proof that employees are indeed your most valuable asset. Define appropriate metrics to measure each behavior and each outcome listed in the job models. Your organization will have many metrics already available, but will probably need to develop new data points in order to gain an adequate snapshot of current levels of behaviors and results.

Collect as much data on behaviors and outcomes as possible, before any actions are taken. It is vitally important that you conduct a baseline measurement of your organizational system before conducting any interventions. This way, you can show the precise effects of change to your systems, enabling you to prove the worth of your projects to your executives and your investors.

Continuously monitor selection-level attribute data, behavioral and outcome data to determine the effect of your interventions. Traditionally, this type of analysis has been performed by Industrial/Organization (I/O) psychologists. Many large firms have an I/O psychologist on staff. These professionals are highly trained in analysis and can often be hired for project work. Some projects prove to be ineffective at producing the desired results, allowing you to eliminate them without further expenditures. Other projects will prove quite beneficial, and thus may be fortified with increased resources.

Refine and update your job models to reflect changes and new understandings. As you move forward, you will be able to refine your model, rendering it more complete and definite as you go. This will allow you to create increasingly concrete arguments for the effectiveness of your interventions. Ultimately, you will be able to make statements such as "a five point improvement in employee attitudes will drive a 1.3 point improvement in customer satisfaction, which in turn will drive a .5 percent improvement in revenue growth." (This is an actual finding from linking competencies to results, quoted in The HR Scorecard, 2001.)

Build a budget that includes investment categories for:

- Job analysis.
- Developing and conducting behavior ratings.
- Data collection and storage.

- Data analysis and reporting.
- Upgrading methods used in evaluating candidates.

Working in a systematic manner, one job at a time, you can add more rigor to your methods, increase the likelihood of hiring more capable performers, and be able to document and report on the numerical consequences of your investments. This will demonstrate the value of HR's contribution "at the table."

EXAMPLE 1. EMPLOYEE BEHAVIOR RATING FORM FOR CUSTOMER CONTACT POSITION

Employee Name: _____

Instructions:

Please use the following scales to describe this employee's behavior on the job. When completing the scales, think about the performance of this employee relative to the other employees in your work group. Try not to rate all of the employees as being the same.

Apply Knowledge: Leverage technical expertise to solve problems; share technical expertise with others; break complex problems down into smaller issues; resolve issues quickly; apply specific knowledge to novel situations. (See Figure 13.2.)

Overall, rate this employee's ability to apply knowledge relative to other employees? (Circle appropriate number.) (See Figure 13.3.)

CHAPTER

14

HR Outsourcing and Metrics

Any modern writing on HR includes some commentary on the prevalence of HR outsourcing (HRO). Since this book is on HR measurement and metrics, this would seem an opportune time to introduce outsourcing here. When writing about HRO and HR metrics the temptation is to list the myriad functional areas, associated measures, and service levels and, while tempting and of possible interest to a few, those looking for that data won't find it in this chapter.

If you're an HR professional looking for benchmarking data on which to make guesstimates on the applicability of outsourcing to your organization, those resources are plentiful . . . elsewhere. This chapter is about the importance of HR measurement in the broader scope of HR service delivery in which outsourcing plays a prominent role.

The Problem

As data supporting the link between human capital and shareholder value has mounted, HR professionals have sought to use this as a way into their organizations' senior leadership teams. But just because prominent HR talking heads espouse that HR deserves a seat at the leadership table doesn't make it so. In spite of the data on their side, HR professionals have a poor track record meeting stakeholders' expectations. No matter how illustrious the strategic thinking, unless the basic needs of the organization are satisfied, HR professionals will not be viewed as competent members of the organizational team.

The goal has been to improve HR's recognition as strategically important at the C-level and become Business Partners, as HR academic and author David Ulrich has proposed. Thus HR's strategy to date has been to minimize the traditional role of administrative, transactional, and resource-intensive processing via outsourcing and instead increase its profile as a business advisor. Each of us has been inundated with the HR "pyramids" used in every PowerPoint presentation at every HR conference. Business leaders expect more than presentations, but to date, the HR community has only been able to talk about what must be done. Our ability to execute this transformation has been slower than executives, shareholders, and, lest we forget, employees would like.

The Failed Promise of Transformation

The most common HR response to elevate their influence in the organization has been to initiate a two-pronged, technology-based program that attempts to remove HR from the bottom of the pyramid while building out the infrastructure that allows them to deliver those services at the top.

Step one: Implement systems to enable "self service" employee and manager transactions to disseminate or outsource the transactional-processing load.

Step two: Implement systems and processes that collect performance and productivity data which, when combined with financial metrics, can be leveraged both in analysis, reporting, and advisory deliverables that mirror their financial counterparts and help to develop and execute strategic decisions.

The current terminology describing HR's new focus is "Human Capital Management," which is perceived as being comparable to financial capital management. This is all well and good, and an appropriate reaction to the well deserved "Personnel" moniker. But as most fads go, outside of self-congratulatory articles, self-promotion, and a few "best practice" exceptions, these initiatives have for the most part failed to achieve their main objective—due in large part to HR's failure to use its own very powerful data in the most effective way. The data alone is not enough; to achieve the status of strategic business advisor HR must consistently demonstrate that its decisions are empirically based, and it must continue to demonstrate a persuasive return-on-investment (ROI) business case.

Quite simply, it is because HR's agenda is based on a fundamentally flawed view of the value that the HR function can and should provide, and on a similarly flawed understanding of how technology-enabled workforce processes can be implemented and managed. The HR function is approaching a crossroads—in most cases HR people are not significantly involved in the business despite their efforts to interlope, and they are unable to derive believable ROI from, or even effectively manage, the enormous complexity of systems and processes that have been implemented.

The Real Value

The central problem is that HR has not explained to its clients the true importance of its mandate. The conventional thinking about HR reflects the paradox facing line managers. If people are the 'most important asset,' why is the HR function often thought of as an administrative overhead? For the most part, this perspective has been justified by the role that HR has played in the past, emphasizing administrative efficiency and compliance. The term "HR police" is not an unjust characterization. The narrow-minded view of "climbing up the pyramid of value" strategy attends to the desire of HR professionals to work on something significant within their organizations, but it fails to address the critical need that companies have to improve the effectiveness of their workforce—a need that HR is uniquely qualified to address. A strategy that continues to focus on the details of administration aims in the wrong direction and will only continue to reinforce the belief that HR people in general just don't understand, or have the capacity to address, the real business of the organization. This strategy of fixed/focusing on HR is doomed to fail because it addresses only a small part of a larger opportunity, and it attempts to deliver only a small portion of the solution.

Though HR owns most people-related functions, it is rarely true that HR is given real responsibility for the effectiveness of the company's people and the company. HR typically has responsibility for people governance, but rarely for the performance of the workforce, and they are almost never an active driver in creating or improving the performance of people's actual work. Instead it fulfills the role of passive provider of an infrastructure for the business to source, select, reward, and deploy its workforce.

To be competitive, most executives are desperately in need of better practices and tools to make their workforce more effective, yet organizational leaders separate HR functions and waste an abundance of data and skill within HR by assigning it the low-priority task of administering the policies and procedures. Look over the shoulder of most workers, and observe the percentage of work affected by the services that HR provides. To optimize that worker's performance requires appropriate training, rewards, and organizational structures—all of which HR has compelling data to inform, and most of which it has the skills to address. Still, it's a safe bet that one will conclude that HR is not a significant participant in the analysis, decision, or execution processes of the business, despite their claims to the contrary, because they simply are too busy performing transactions, or because they are not taken seriously by frontline workers, managers, and executives as business experts who will add value or as real businesspeople who can make a bottom line difference. It hurts to say it, but it's true, and it will hurt even more to continue to be essentially useless. Instead, HR is seen as the corporate police, the rule-enforcers, the people who take the handbook seriously, and the people who will make you follow the standard process if you let them get involved.

That said, HR is the only function within a company that is reasonably positioned to improve the way people work. HR owns and manages all of the data about workers and work: their jobs, expertise, organizations, backgrounds, skills, requirements, and compensation structure. HR as a discipline—not the department—has a matchless understanding of the factors that govern worker productivity: competencies, management processes, relationships, rewards, collaboration, learning, job structures, partnership models, and more. Every action a worker takes can potentially be improved by the data HR has about them and their work, or by the expertise HR has about how to productively organize the workforce and the work. HR's attention and influence are usually restricted to administrative duties; not improving the performance of the "real" work that should be a reflection of HR's priorities. It should be obvious that, while HR's strategy of improvement through self-service and competency analyses and historical turnover reporting may be marginally useful, it is usually the case that higher value work improvements need to be addressed first and should be HR's focus. No other function within the organization is able to address this critical need. Information Technology (IT) often inherits this role simply because technology is everywhere, and is a key enabling resource in getting work done. However, IT typically does not have the skill set to improve the efficiency and effectiveness of work processes, implement consistent policies, or deliver a work environment that take full advantage of relevant knowledge, resources, and tools. IT is accountable for the efficiency of the architecture from a systems perspective, which is why so many promising initiatives have such surprisingly inefficient long-term results. Most fail to achieve what they promise because they are not effectively integrated to support work processes. Only HR is responsible for knowing and managing how the workforce should work.

Line management is also not well matched to define and manage overall worker effectiveness. Operations staff do not typically have the expertise in configuring organizations or work processes, managing and distributing knowledge, or the talent to manage or integrate the necessary enterprise-wide and external resources. HR has the data and the expertise about the workforce and the perspective about the overall work environment. Each facet of what a company does can be improved by this expertise. This improvement will lead directly and measurably to bottom-line business results as more and more financial studies confirm.

All of the preceding merely confirms what most of us have known intuitively for a long time: The results a company achieves are directly proportional to the efficacy of its people in developing and executing the company's core business. Worker effectiveness is determined, broadly speaking, by the organization, available knowledge and tools.

HR outsourcing and metrics seem inexorably linked together. For HR to lead the development and implementation workforce strategies in support of organizational objectives, they must relinquish their transactional processing role. When combined with a strong HRO partner(s), HR can upgrade its service delivery and access to HR and workforce performance measures.

Integrated HR Outsourcing

HRO is the outsourcing of an integrated group of HR processes to an external partner. Typically the contract combines systems, end-to-end processes, HR staff, and infrastructure. HRO got off to a flying start in the late 90s with a series of landmark deals by major players, including BP Amoco, Nortel Networks, BT, and BAE Systems. Given the pivotal and pervasive role of HR, the choice between HRO and an in-house solution should be based on much more than a comparison of costs. Some observers claim that integrated HRO is intrinsically more difficult than other kinds of outsourcing. Others say that any lull in the double digit growth rates of HRO is an inevitable and natural hiatus between early adopters and mainstream acceptance, and that the HRO market is exhibiting many of the evolutionary characteristics seen in the initial stages of today's more mature forms of outsourcing, like during IT outsourcing's early days in the 1980s. Both analyses have some merit. But whichever of them is closer to the truth, the consensus now is that the trend for HRO is upwards.

While many early HR outsourcing agreements were based solely on the projected cost savings for the client, today's outsourcing contracts should be based on the strategic value of the outsourcing relationship. In some cases, outsourcing may not fit with strategic goals. This is why it is imperative that, before embarking on an HR outsourcing arrangement, organizations achieve a solid understanding of costs and human resources service requirements. The first step should involve a sourcing diagnostic, which is an evaluation of the current state of HR in the organization. The sourcing diagnostic will result in a snapshot, capturing how and where the HR department is allocating its resources, in terms of people, process, and technology. The second step should be an examination of the HR department's business objectives, along with a determination of the best ways to deliver on those objectives, either by outsourcing all or some HR components, or by not outsourcing anything. It is important to remember that, while outsourcing is one service delivery model, it is not the only one.

Metrics Can Play a Pivotal Role in HR Outsourcing Success or Failure

1. *Over-optimism among companies looking to outsource HR.* Expectations have been pitched unrealistically high, both in terms of cost savings and service improvements, and the speed at which these can be realized. Though cost savings can be front-loaded to bring immediate financial benefit, the process of bedding down the new service and integrating HR technologies may take upwards of 18 months from the start of the contract.

2. *Poor knowledge of the baseline.* Management is often ill-informed about the direct and indirect costs of existing HR processes and practices, and about how HR costs are embedded within the organization. HR personnel themselves often only have a tenuous grasp on the true end-to-end processes, as line management handles so many people-related activities. These shortcomings have resulted in poorly defined business cases that fail to identify the true costs and true implications of outsourcing.

3. *Poor supplier management and performance metrics.* Companies have often entrusted HRO to poorly structured "supply management units," staffed by HR professionals unfamiliar with complex supplier relationships. Frequently the effect is to put the supplier in the driving seat rather than the customer. Performance metrics may also be inappropriate, focusing on a confusing array of operational and cost savings while ignoring value creation goals. Metrics are also often made up on the run when the outsourcing contract is already up and running and its success under threat.

What Is the Measure of Reward for Getting It Right?

If handled well, HRO has the proven capability to deliver three transformational benefits:

1. *Cost reduction.* The cost benefits fall into three categories—direct costs, future investment, and the hidden costs of existing service inefficiencies.

   - HRO reduces the *direct costs* of HR service provision, with an organization typically saving around 20 percent of its existing cost base when it outsources HR transactional services. This level of savings builds up over the first two years of the deal and is generally guaranteed by the supplier—which will also offer the customer the option of negotiating either a flat savings profile across the life of the deal or a front-loaded profile. Greater cost savings can be gained if the organization is prepared to extend the contract to 10 years, accept a highly automated 'vanilla' service suite, and/or allow some off-shoring to a low-cost geography.

   - HRO removes the burden of *future investment* in HR systems and infrastructure. This can save a large organization tens of millions of dollars—basically the cost of creating a professional HR services platform complete with telephone call center services and case management system, HR tools for training and for recruiting, a self-service portal and an HRIS such as 'SAP.' The vendor will usually supply an HR platform consisting of these elements automatically under the agreement.

- HRO reduces the *hidden costs* of current HR service ineffi-ciencies. This benefit is delivered by:

  - Process harmonization and automation.

  - Better forecasting of demand.

  - Elimination of errors through "Six Sigma" quality initiatives.

  - Savings on third-party spend, like recruitment agency fees or car fleet costs. Most large organizations have hundreds of vendors and suppliers providing services via the HR department. The ability to rationalize and re-duce that number is a prime goal of HR outsourcing. Vendors typically estimate additional savings of around 10 percent from this area.

2. *Improved infrastructure.* HRO brings the organization access to new technologies and usually a vastly superior HR services platform. Self-service functionality—in the form of an HR portal backed up by a shared service center, providing the workforce with a single point of contact for HR administra-tion—is an attractive proposition, especially for organiza-tions facing an uphill struggle to secure the investment to build this internally, or struggling to find the skills and capa-bilities to implement it. Outsourcing providers bring to bear cutting-edge technology and an integrated delivery of HR services based on the employee work/life cycle, rather than "stove pipe" processes. Added bonuses include improved re-porting and analytics to measure performance and return on investment.

3. *New HR operational model.* When designing a new HR opera-tional model either for in-house implementation or HRO, the key to maximizing efficiency lies in radically reshaping HR's service delivery around an HR shared services center (SSC). Experience shows that the impact of a successful HR

SSC can be dramatic. Barclays Bank's in-house HR SSC, implemented in 2000, achieved its targets of HR service transformation and a near-50 percent cost saving by the start of 2003. BAEO Systems' outsourced solution delivered a guaranteed reduction in HR transaction costs of 10 percent in the first year and 15 percent in the second, with expected savings of 50 percent within five years. So the choice facing organizations is clear: should we build and own this shared service engine? Or should we rent capacity from a third-party outsourcer?

With an in-house solution, the benefits include the potential for the organization to exercise greater direct control over the continuous improvement of HR processes and service levels, and a closer relationship between HR and the rest of the business. The organization will also own all HR intellectual property and know-how, plus the HR SSC asset. However, these benefits are balanced by a number of potential drawbacks. The cost of ownership will be high, plus will not be offset by the economies of scale that an outsource provider enjoys. Management questions may arise over whether owning—and investing in—an HR SSC is sufficiently core to justify being a wholly owned part of the business. And an in-house HR SSC can give rise to a clash between HR's role as an efficient factory for HR transactions and its ability to act as a trusted adviser to the business.

Know Your Business—and Know Outsourcing

So, what do decision-makers need to do when facing a choice over the right route to HR transformation? Clearly, HR transformation can be achieved via either HRO or in-house development, with the key differences being issues of asset ownership, investment, and control. First of all management must develop an all around view of what each of these two options would mean for the organization in financial, managerial, cultural, and value terms. This involves taking a long, hard look at the organization's managerial and financial resources, at what it will need to deliver its commercial strategy, and at the role that either an HRO or in-house solution might play in meeting those requirements.

In conducting this feasibility study, management can draw some valuable object lessons, both from recent successes and from the failure of a number of earlier HR BPO projects. Prior practical experience of HRO is also valuable—and an organization with a successful track record of HRO in other functions such as IT or finance is likely to be better placed to implement HRO successfully. However, of all types of outsourcing, HR is probably the most difficult and sensitive because of HR's combination of transactional and advisory processes, its pervasive role, and its potential impact on staff morale and performance.

This consideration underlines the central fact about deciding whether to outsource HR: It is not a choice that should be made purely on grounds of short-term costs. To make the right long-term decision, management must know what the organization needs from HR, how HRO works, and what will happen when these two elements are fused together. Costs matter—but so do service quality, management, and culture.

Fast Company Came Close ... Tom Stewart Came Closer

In a 1996 article for *Fortune*, "Taking on the Last Bureaucracy," Tom Stewart suggested companies should, in a phrase, "blow the sucker up," referring to HR departments. Given the way HR was conducting its business at that time, Stewart thought the HR function of people management might be better served by non-HR departments in an organization. But in fact, Stewart was slightly off base. It's not the HR departments that need to be blown up. It's the wall that HR has erected between itself and the rest of a company's business that needs to be obliterated.

Glancing through the HR and business press, you'll find a proliferation of articles extolling the value of human capital and human capital management. In the past several years, both the frequency and fervor of these messages have grown and with good reason. The intuitive sense executives at some of the world's most successful organizations have had for years—the same sense that has driven them to create the "good place to work" status widely coveted by organizations and widely covered in list upon list in the business press—now is supported by overwhelming quantitative evidence, that is, that the right alignment of human resource practices to business strategy can add shareholder value. There are numerous studies, such as those done by PA Consulting, Watson Wyatt, along with Huselid and Becker, on human capital effectiveness that argue successfully that:

- Business congruent human-capital practices are leading indicators of financial performance. Quantitative data indicates that effective human-capital practices drive positive business outcomes more than positive business outcomes lead to good HR practices. Human capital initiatives implemented now will help companies convalesce faster and emerge stronger when the economy eventually rebounds.

- Shareholder returns at companies with business congruent human-capital practices are at least three times those at companies with disconnected practices. During the economic expansion of the 90s, that performance was significant, but not nearly as large. The lesson learned is that it's even more important to focus on human-capital superiority in tough times.

- Human-capital practices are not created equally. There are those that create substantial value and others that actually diminish it. Companies must examine their HR initiatives to ensure they are adding to shareholder value.

Still, very few individuals outside the field of HR seem to be buying this message outright, leaving HR in the awkward position of justifying a place for themselves on the leadership team. In part, this is because an artificial wall has been erected between HR and "operations," a wall that continues to exist in large part because of the attitudes and practices of HR professionals themselves. HR professionals, in their headlong dash from the despair of the duties comprising their current responsibility, have rushed past their most powerful trump card: the people. All organizations—private, public, nonprofit, service, manufacturing—are composed of people. Everything that any company produces, all of the value created, is achieved through the actions of those people. Simply put, the effectiveness of a company is inextricably dependent on the effectiveness of its people.

15

A Practical Guide to Building Your Ultimate Dashboard

What will your ultimate HR dashboard look like? I hope that it will look different from every other organization's ultimate dashboard, since your organization's priorities and service level with executives will be different from those of other organizations. But, how do you determine what it will look like? How do you convert the metrics into digestible, actionable data points that will assist the executive team in managing the organization? What are the usual pitfalls that you may encounter in building your reports and your dashboard? What practical advice do best-practitioners have for building your ultimate dashboard?

How to Develop Your Ultimate Dashboard

Setting Your Goals. Each measure in the dashboard should have a goal or target. Compile management interviews, Human Resources priorities, and set the measurement goal against the desired performance for the organization. Ideally, you will be able to determine a hard dollar amount of savings or revenue increase from the goal (such as decreasing turnover by 10 percent results in a $5 million annual savings), or you will be able to tie back a stated executive priority (such as, We promote a culture of promoting from within).

Modeling Your Measures. You have already determined what the executive's priorities are, and now you need to model what the metric will look like. What data will you need? What best practices exist that are appropriate for this measure? Model your metric using mock data in Excel and shop it around to others for feedback. Make sure to validate your decisions.

Building Your Metrics. This is the actual work of creating the metric using real data. If you have an ad hoc tool this could be user-accessible; if not, you may need the support of a technical resource to build the reports for you. If you do need a technical resource, modeling the metrics becomes critical to your success since your report developer needs to understand exactly what the report is supposed to do.

Building Your Dashboard. Think of your dashboard as a collection of well-focused reports on one page. After you have your reports created, you can begin think about how best to represent them on a single page using graphs and other elaborate techniques where necessary.

Caring for Your Data. You may have the information you need in many different places. Someone needs to care for this data, which includes making sure that users of the technology supporting you (HRIS, ATS, TMS, and so on) are completing the information you need. This also includes surveys. A little maintenance of the data saves hours of data repair later on.

Validating Your Results. Without validation, your organization could easily be representing your data in the completely wrong way. Check your assumptions with your peers, with managers in different departments, or even finance. Gerry Crispin of Career Xroads tells a remarkable story about a young HR manager who wanted to completely change the way the company recruited, but she didn't know how to build the ROI case and didn't know how to get the data she needed. So, she approached the COO and asked for help. Not only did he help her create the ROI with all of the supporting data, but he co-presented the idea to the board, and the two of them completely changed the way the company approached recruiting for the better.

Communicating Your Ultimate Dashboard

You already know what a great dashboard looks like if you happen to drive a car. When you are considering how to design your dashboard, keep your car's dashboard in mind. It's simple. It gives you important information by scanning it quickly. It tells you when there is danger or when you should accelerate. Great dashboards are visual representations of data used to make important decisions.

Making a great dashboard is not easy. There are people who dedicate their entire lives to representing data clearly, elegantly, and simply. For an in-depth look at different ways of representing your data, explore Edward Tufte's books, including *The Visual Display of Quantitative Information* (www.edwardtufte.com), and W. Bradford Paley's work seen at http://textarc.org. These will give you a few ideas on how to represent and clearly communicate your data:

Stoplights. Stoplights are a traditional project manager's tool to convey risk in projects. Using red, yellow, green highlights on your metrics can immediately communicate visually how the organization is performing against goals without much need for explanation on the page, which make them ideal for a dashboard. Figure 15.1 shows an example of the stoplight approach as applied to Intel's HR metrics (see Chapter 13 for more on Intel's dashboard).

Progress Against Goals. Showing metrics without context creates more difficult executive meetings—you have not provided them

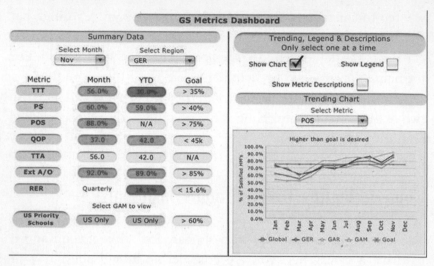

Figure 15.1

with the information that they need to help move the HR agenda forward. What is required is a key indicator on each of the metrics provided in the dashboard. An example from Dr. John Sullivan, the head of Human Management at San Francisco State University (Sullivan 2002) is shown in Table 15.1.

Gauges. Just like stoplights, gauges are an easy-to-understand way to convey current performance information and the goal of

Table 15.1

Metric	Last Year	3 Months	3 Month Recurring Average	Current	Warning Level
New hire performance (based on performance-appraisal scores at 6 months) on scale of 0 to 5, 5 being highest	3.4	3.6	3.78	3.65	3.5
Time-to-productivity in days	45	42	44	43	45
Turnover rate of top performers	6.8%	4.7%	4.9%	5.1%	3%

that information. Readers intuitively understand gauges from driving automobiles or simply from reading the temperature. Gauges for dashboards can be used to interpret complex data in one visual. In the example in Figure 15.2, the needle is indicating the current value of the metric. The range of average values is represented by the larger rectangle the needle is sitting in, and the top rectangle represents the goal for the metric (www.dundas.com).

Combining Notes, Tables, and Visuals. Most dashboards have a combination of tables and graphics. Managing to balance the dashboard and notating the data appropriately is a true art. When creating the visual dashboard, try splitting up your page with two columns: one column should take two-thirds of the page; the other data will populate the other third of the page. Many times, this layout works for visual representations of your data since it allows you to display time-based line graphs if needed and show a few months of data. Long bar charts will have the same result.

Notice in Figure 15.3 that many of the data items have notes attached to them, but they do not overwhelm the dashboard. You may not immediately notice that the notes are there at all. After meeting with your executive team a few times, you may begin to build an intuition as to what types of information they tend to ask about, or what departments they'll tend to question the data on. Build easy-to-find notes right into the dashboard. This will make communication of the core data much easier.

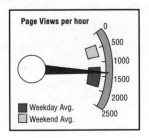

Figure 15.2

December 2000 Recruiting Scorecard

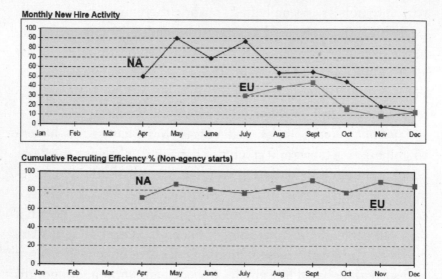

Monthly New Hire Activity

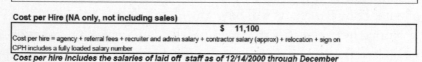

Cumulative Recruiting Efficiency % (Non-agency starts)

Cost per Hire (NA only, not including sales)

	$ 11,100

Cost per hire = agency + referral fees + recruiter and admin salary + contractor salary (approx) + relocation + sign on
CPH includes a fully loaded salary number

Cost per hire includes the salaries of laid off staff as of 12/14/2000 through December

Figure 15.3

Best Dashboard Practices with Scott Morrison, Manager of Recruiting Programs at Salesforce.com

What is on your Ultimate Executive Dashboard?

The bottom line in our organization is our candidate pipeline. We're a Customer Relationship Management company, so we think about our talent metrics like our sales pipeline. Our executives want to know what talent will we be closing in 30, 60, and 90 days. They want to know about Time-to-Start and about New Hire Quality. We can track all of this well since most of our users are using our own CRM tools. Hiring Manager Satisfaction is also important to us as is exit-interview data with candidates. We should do more with cost management and optimization, which will be coming in the future. We do use competitive data as well to emphasize areas we're excelling at, and the areas we need to work on.

How frequently do you meet with the CEO on data?
We meet almost weekly. We have aggressive goals, and the C-level executive wants to see how we're doing.

What is on your Ultimate HR-Centric Dashboard?
It's a granular view of our executive data. We want to show our teams here exactly what executives expect of our teams. For the recruiters, we manage to a talent pipeline from "req to check" and hone in on the weak points across the entire staffing process. Interview pipelines by department, talent pools are critical for us.

What was the most interesting thing you learned from analyzing data on your talent base?
Our employees are so talented. We've done a ton of analysis in understanding skills and interests so we can really maximize the great people we have. There is so much opportunity here for organizations like us.

What would be your best piece of advice for building a great dashboard?
Don't overlook the "coolness factor" of the dashboard—displaying the data visually to executives gets them excited, even if the data is really kind of boring.

How to Make Really Big Mistakes

Mistake One: Dashboard clutter. Don't mistake using a dashboard with the idea of "cramming as much data on one page as is humanly possible for my executive to see." Experienced managers of data know that the dashboard is your instrument panel that will assist you (or an executive) in making decisions based on the gauges and indicators on the dashboard. You're designing your instrument panel for making decisions. Don't clutter it up with data you won't make a decision with.

Mistake Two: Right report, wrong cut of data. You can easily have the right columns and the right rows, but it is entirely possible to make a mistake when selecting what data to use in the report. For example, your executives want to see a real-time view of all open requisitions. However, when you run your report, you select all jobs opened within the month, not all jobs currently open as of the date of the report being run. The difference can be huge. You may have opened up only 10 jobs in March, but on March 30 there are 100 jobs open. While this example is pretty obvious, others are sinisterly difficult to detect. Think about the following cuts of the same data and what they tell you on a report of interview statuses. What is the difference when you select all interview statuses where:

- Only jobs that were *closed* within the month are reported?
- Only interview statuses that *occurred* in the month are reported?
- Only jobs that were *opened* within the month are reported?
- Only jobs that are *open right now* are reported?
- Only the *final statuses of candidates* in closed jobs are reported?

If your head is spinning, you are not alone. All five choices are completely legitimate—and all five choices answer very different questions. Reporting interview statuses on all closed jobs will give you a clear historic picture of how candidates wind their way through the interview process, allowing you to see average time between important interview stages. Reporting on statuses that occurred in a month gives you a picture of what work a recruiter did during the month. A final status report will report on how your candidates looked at their last status, which could actually be your applicant flow log.

It's the same report, but it has a very different meaning depending on what data you select. How do you avoid the problem? Before you run your data, make sure you know what you want the report to tell you. And then check your query to make sure you're grabbing the right data!

Mistake Three: Not articulating a clear business problem that the metric will answer. Every element on your dashboard must have a relevant question that you can use to sum up why that metric is being run. Test it for yourself on your current metrics. If you can write down exactly what question the metric answers, then you have a clear metric with a clear goal. Example: "I want to monitor learning and development expenditures in real time so I can intervene before the month ends to make sure that we didn't overspend on sales training and underspend on management training." You can definitely build a metric around that articulated business question. *At all costs, avoid reporting on a metric merely because you have it available!*

Mistake Four: Trying to accomplish too many goals with one report. A surefire way to tie up several days of thought is to try to make one report do too many things. You will add columns, improve some data, and hurt other data. We've all been sucked down the quicksand of a reporting challenge—being drawn in further and further to fix the problem that the last addition to the report created until you wind up with a report that doesn't make sense. If you feel you're spinning your wheels, stop. Back up. Reapproach your original goal.

Mistake Five: Believing that your data is a complete picture of reality. Some of what you are going to report is not black and white data. Even finance has to make decisions about reporting that fall into grey areas; certainly Human Resources is in the same situation. You may need to make choices on how to represent your data that isn't exactly how it happened in real life. For instance, HR runs an ad for 15 different positions in 9 different departments. If you run a department level cost analysis of recruiting expenses, you are likely going to need to make a decision on how to divide up those expenses. Even if you have a method for handling this, it is still an approximation of reality at the department level. As long as you can accurately describe your assumptions to anyone that needs to understand the data, you have done well.

Dealing with Bad Data

Every manager of data struggles with the same problem: bad data. It's not just the Human Resources function. We have even coined a favorite phrase for it—GIGO: Garbage in, garbage out. Bad data can't be the excuse not to present the needed metrics to a hiring manager or an executive or your own teams. If everyone has the problem, then there must be workarounds to dealing with bad data so that you can use it in your reporting without ill effect. There are a few different classes of bad data to manage:

Incomplete data. Every report on the planet will eventually have one row of data that isn't included. It's okay. What's not okay is not being aware of what you don't have. If you are reporting voluntary turnover and you cannot get that information from a newly acquired entity, then make sure it's clearly noted on your dashboard. You'll probably get some executive intervention so that next time the data hole is patched.

Inaccurate data. Time-to-Start metrics have this problem all the time. Somehow, after running the data the first time, you find that your average time to start is -34 days because recruiters were taking out reqs after the candidate was identified and hired. You can intervene to fix the process *and* fix the data. Beware of using averages with inaccurate data. One practical method of repairing the data to get at least an approximation of Time-to-Start is to remove the offending rows. If you find that your time to fill is -34 days, look through the rows and start eliminating all of the negative Time-to-Fill and 0-days-to-fill rows. A more accurate (though not exact) Time-to-Start will emerge.

Technical problems in relating the data. Sometimes you have lots of data in lots of places. You try to join that data together by using Microsoft Access and a common field (say employee number), but you don't get what you expect. This is a problem in relating the two data sets together and can definitely set you back hours (or days) if you do not have the technical background. When you are in this predicament, stop as quickly as you can and get help. In the right hands, this problem can be fixed quickly.

What Is a Data Warehouse?

Technology types (the authors included) love to use opaque terms for pretty simple concepts. You may have heard of the term "data warehouse" or "data mart." We will define them both in the context of reporting. Your IT people don't like running reports directly against your HRIS and other production systems that lots of people need to use at the same time. Reports slow down systems. It's also inefficient to run reports off these systems for a few technical reasons.

A data mart is a more compact version of a portion of the data in your HRIS, ATS, or other production system. The data mart is dedicated just to reporting. It has no other purpose. This takes the pressure off your live systems to satisfy your reporting needs and allow other users to do the work of HR (adding employees, employee self-service, and so on). Think of a data warehouse as a collection of data marts all working together. If you have data from 10 different systems and you want to report on all of them, likely your IT team will talk about building a data warehouse. Your organization may have data stored in a talent management system, HRIS, benefits system, or performance management system. Data warehouses need to be carefully planned, so the more you know about the metrics you need to report, the better, cheaper, and faster a data warehouse can be built and be useful to your organization.

Best Dashboard Practices with Mary Claire Ryan, Director of Sourcing at Riviera Advisors

How do you ensure that the data you present is the data that is important to your CEO?

Before I begin to think about the data, I use an in-depth questionnaire and sit with the CEO to understand his/her priorities. Even with that set of meetings, I know there will be a surprise in every meeting I have subsequently, whether it's a business shift, entering a new product line, or an acquisition—process to dig into the new initiatives, business realities, and so on.

What is on your Ultimate Executive Dashboard?

The first data points on my dashboard are related to Workforce Planning in the short term and in the long term. I map the key initiatives, new priorities, and economic realities to a practical talent plan for the organization. This is not a typical "telephone book" sized workforce plan—it's concise, forward-looking, and has red flags where I think executives need to pay attention.

Then I'll keep the key data points that we've worked out with the executive team. Usually, turnover, New Hire Quality, and talent budgeting will be on the dashboard. A review of talent targets will be on there too, including management targets, internal survey data, and hiring manager feedback.

I also always have a nugget of competitive information as well to compare us to, and I don't hold back. If we're not keeping up with talent acquisition, or if our competitor snapped up the top engineers in our most profitable business unit, executives will know about it.

How frequently do you meet with the CEO on data?

I never bother the C-level until I have hard facts on the data that's important to them. Then, I make sure my executives are armed with the two to three key data points they need for board meetings, investor calls, and their employee talks.

What is on your Ultimate HR-Centric Dashboard?

I've focused on using data to manage both dedicated recruiters, which require a specific set of data to manage versus generalists that are also responsible for recruiting in the organization. I'll focus on the generalists here with respect to recruiting.

I tend to focus on the recruiting process immediately when managing a team of generalists since it tends to have plenty of management opportunities for improvement. Hiring Manager Satisfaction data is important to me. It helps me show the team exactly what our constituents expect of us and where we are at. I'll also compile our own performance reviews focusing on key areas like sales skills in recruiting candidates through the interview process.

In addition, I also like to look at our commitments to our hiring managers with a strong focus on Time-to- Start (not time to hire), New Hire Quality, and Candidate Interview Feedback. I also try to arm my generalists with data that assists them in educating their hiring managers on market forces in recruiting, candidate lag, and the hiring manager's own responsiveness.

What was the most interesting thing you have learned from analyzing data on your talent base?

Here's an example that shocked executives inside and outside of HR. We were having a terrible problem hiring for a highly-skilled, highly-degreed job group that was critical to profitability in our core business. First, we took a look at the external market and found our first problem: 80 percent of the candidates with the skill sets we needed lived across the country, nowhere near us. Then, we did an analysis of the population of potential candidates and found our shocker—we already employed 50 percent of the candidates with the degree we were looking for! They were working in a completely different division, doing a job that didn't actually require the degree and skill sets we needed. The employees were underutilized in their current job, while another business line was suffering. We presented a plan to offer a great internal mobility opportunity to these employees and a plan to train other potential candidates to fill their old jobs. It was a win-win plan that was directly tied to business outcomes and talent optimization.

What is your best piece of advice in building a great dashboard?

Keep it simple at first! Make sure you don't try to use one report to tell three stories. Tell one story and make it a good one with clean data.

Where to Leverage Technology

The cost of collecting data. What is the actual cost of collecting all of the needed data? Your labor and dollar cost will vary, but the cost is at least 10 times less expensive today than it was 15 years ago. Specifically, costs have gone down because:

- HRIS and ATS systems are better able to provide data quickly.
- Survey tools are now web-enabled and accessible directly by Human Resources with less expertise needed to develop.
- Data collection from the staffing function has improved as Talent Management Systems have made it easier to status and rank candidates (recruiters now can batch status scores of candidates at the same time).

- New technologies that were designed to automate processes also give managers greater visibility. For example, if you have just implemented performance reviews online, you can likely now run a report on the top 10 percent of performers by department in 2005. How long did it take to compile that data by hand in 1999?

What to do when you do not have a dedicated analyst running your metrics. Many of us don't have an HRIS analyst dedicated to creating and running complex reports and then assembling them into dashboards. If there is a provable ROI, hiring that analyst and/or outsourcing the compilation is a good investment. However, when you are directly challenged to provide a dashboard, with limited time and limited resources, do the following things:

Keep it simple, stupid. Focus on fewer metrics and fewer data points. Make sure that your data is cleaned well and focuses on displaying your data simply using tables, pivot tables, or pivot charts.

Use the most of PowerPoint and Excel. Both have many flaws. However, quickly displaying information visually isn't one of them. If you are crunched for time and resources, use PowerPoint to lay out your dashboard and Excel to create your charts and/or pivot tables or pivot charts.

Find your high-potential in HR. There is inevitably one high-potential in Human Resources that loves to dig into data, knows Excel very well, and is fearless. Find this high-potential and harness his/her energy for the dashboard project.

Ad hoc reporting. The words "ad hoc" are generally not used correctly in HR. Many times, people use the words ad hoc to describe real time reporting. Or, ad hoc means "I can run whatever I want whenever I want, and however I want to show it." Neither of these definitions is particularly true. Ad hoc reporting systems are amazing tools when you know what service they provide.

A true ad hoc reporting environment (like Brio, Crystal, or Microsoft reporting services) provides business-level users with the ability to create relationships between their data, pick fields, build calculations, and create reports without (necessarily) the use of a technology resource. Ad hoc environments put the data in the hands of the business user. Most ad hoc reporting environments are not run against real-time data but against a data warehouse or another snapshot of the data. Ad hoc environments have constraints against what they can and can't run. And all ad hoc reporting systems require the business user not only to learn the sophisticated software but also to be comfortable with the data and the tables that store them.

What are ad hoc reports capable of providing to HR? Actually, quite a lot. However, that doesn't cure all of the problems of reporting. In fact, it introduces a few more concerns.

Ad hoc reports still need to be planned out and tested against the source data precisely. It's far too easy to create a report that one believes is reporting average tenure of staff in the sales team, and then find out that a small error in the ad hoc report has been over-reporting the information by months. When using an ad hoc report, here's what you should expect it to provide and what you should not expect it to provide. Expect that ad hoc reports will:

- Run simple tables, selecting the fields that you're looking for, row by row.
- Summarize information in pivot table-type reports.
- Turn cells red or yellow or green in stoplight fashion if a measure exceeds a threshold.
- Create some graphics based on the data (although perhaps not exactly how you've envisioned them).
- Schedule the reports to be sent out to colleagues automatically.

Generally, *do not* depend on your ad hoc system to:

- Check your data for correctness. Humans created the report, Humans need to validate them.

- Control a dashboard display to a very fine degree. Some systems can accomplish this with the assistance of a specialist in the software. But out of the box, a beginner probably would have a hard time here.

- Do acrobatic tricks. This type of software allows a user to do a great deal without technical help. But it also means that the user is constrained by the templates and tools the reporting system provides. Without technical help, it may not be able to put the exact graphic in the exact spot with the exact result that you're looking to produce.

- When setting up the dashboard using ad hoc tools, working with a software expert is a good investment when possible.

Conclusion

Though this section brings the book to a close, the story of metrics is far from over; before anyone can discuss new and better metrics, it is essential to take the lessons from this book and apply them to your organization. As with our analogy on the development of measuring longitude, HR metrics are essential to the success of an organization. Thus, it is important to understand the dynamics of metrics, which this book has broken down and examined. While we would like to stress the significance of every point this book makes, there are several key points that, at the very least, can serve as a starting point in your quest to develop and implement metrics within your organization.

Business strategies must be considered when building metrics; however, they are not the ultimate arbitrator. It is imperative that the human capital deliverables have a concrete impact on the business strategy. Nevertheless, when developing metrics for your organization, they should be aligned with the objectives, not the strategy. Anybody can design a strategy; the real challenge lies in creating objectives. Once objectives are in place, developing strategy not only becomes easier, it becomes more focused.

It is especially important for HR to be able to incorporate and align itself with the organization-wide mission and objectives. This is because most C-level executives do not believe that HR is currently aligned, particularly when compared with other departments such as accounting. What do these departments have that HR lacks? For one, other departments, or at least as they are perceived, have a better understanding of the corporate goals and therefore are able to match every procedure with those goals. There is a need for HR to establish a strong correlation between human capital and the organization's objectives.

The motivation for gathering metrics should not come from a desire to have numbers to present at the next executive meeting. Rather they should come from the need to answer the following question: What decision will this metric support? There are literally thousands of decisions made daily by organizations. In order to make sure the correct decisions are made, a decision support system needs to be in place. There are many aspects that help support decisions, including the decision maker(s) themselves.

One of the most common business decision practices involves a cost and benefits analysis. Thus, it is necessary to apply this concept to human capital. This is of particular significance today because, for most organizations in the modern economy, human capital is the single most costly but also most valuable asset they can claim as their own. There are numerous models that attempt to measure the contribution of employees in terms of both production and knowledge. Understanding the positive contributions that employees give an organization must, of course, be weighed against the risks that these employees pose to the organization. Risks, defined as the odds of a negative impact upon objectives, have a broad range of categories. They can be insurable or noninsurable; can have a measurable price tag or be an abstract figure. Regardless of all the various types of risks, as well as ways to quantify risk profiles; this puts the organization in an advantageous position, should something negative or even catastrophic occur.

Understanding the cost and benefits of human capital is a valuable principle to be aware of before wading into the pool of metrics. Another concept that should be thoroughly understood is the ability to understand what other C-level executives want from HR. As mentioned before, aligning the department's missions and objectives with those of the entire organization is fundamental. However, it is equally important to be able to run the department based on that vision. The employee lifecycle provides management with a framework to work with when applying metrics. The employee lifecycle consists of the following five stages: Attract → Acquire → Develop → Utilize → Separate. Each of the stages is equally important.

Each stage of the employee lifecycle should be measured. However, it is not enough to measure them without the mission and objectives in place. This is a constant point that needs to be reiterated. Mission, objectives, and metrics are the three most important facets of successful human resourcing. Knowing and understanding all dimensions of the Human Capital Blueprint™ helps management to build the missions, objectives, and metrics.

Hiring remains one of the most critical functions of Human Resources, and the need to measure these procedures is paramount. This book stresses not only the need to measure but also to measure correctly—that is, using the right metrics, namely New Hire Quality, Time, Hiring Manager Satisfaction, Recruiting Cost Ratio (RCR), and Recruiting Efficiency. When using the final two metrics, it is important to remember that RCR is the ultimate budgeting and resource allocation tool while Recruiting Efficiency is a comparison tool; the two should not be confused.

According to the 2006 Recruiting Metrics and Performance Benchmark Report, nearly 70 percent of employees cite "professional development learning" as the reason they desire to switch employers. Thus, there is a clear correlation between employee development and retention. How well your organization fares with these concepts can only be known for sure with proper metrics. Being able to develop and retain the employees you want to keep is a key function for HR and is invariably linked to the success of the organization.

A key part of professional development lies in utilizing the skills an employee learns following training, education, or any other type of development that is given. Using metrics to identify the candidates whom your organization most values as future leaders can result in more efficient use of training and development dollars. While policies concerning succession planning and internal mobility are necessary, it is the program as a whole that is best measured.

A key reason for measuring employee performance is because it is so closely tied with organizational performance. That is why metrics must be tied to the mission and objectives of the organization. Employee performance is the result of attributes and performance. Understanding this and of course the organization's mission and objectives will help you find measures of meaning—ones that both HR and executives can respond to.

Often, however, there are measures that, no matter how important they are to the HR function, executives simply do not have time to hear about. Creating a dashboard solves this problem by summarizing and displaying only the most relevant information, including measures and the respective goals. Your dashboard, like those found in cars, should present data in a simple fashion. Constructing an effective dashboard will help executives to understand the current state of an organization's human resources.

The dynamics of human capital continue to evolve. However, performance and success will always be linked. The ability to maximize the performance of your human assets relies on the ability to measure their attributes; exploit the strengths, and examine the weaknesses. In the perilous sea of business, is your organization navigating with longitude or is it merely drifting? Without the proper measurement tools, your organization is risking its own existence, competing with organizations that measure, correctly and on time. Measurement arms organizations with a competitive advantage and it is imperative to take it. We have provided you with the framework—it is now up to you to implement metrics into your organization.

References

ANSI (American National Standards Institute). 1999. ANSI Public Document Library.

ANSI (American National Standards Institute). 2006. ANSI Overview.

APA (American Psychological Association). 1999. *The standards for educational and psychological testing.* Washington, DC: APA.

Arveson, P. 1999. *Translating performance metrics from the private to the public sector.* Washington, D.C.: Balanced Scorecard Institute.

Barber, F., and R. Stack. 2005. *The surprising economics of a "people business." Harvard Business Review* (June).

Barber, J. 2004. The numbers game: Nine steps to making the most of your HR metrics. *IntroNet* 4.

Blair, M., and S. Wallan. Understanding intangible sources of value. Brookings Project, The Brookings Institution.

Bossidy, L., and R. Charam. 2002. *Execution: The discipline of getting things done.* New York: Crown Business.

Boudreau, J.W., and P.M. Ramstad. 2001. From professional business partner to strategic talent leader: What's next for human resources management. CAHRS Working Paper Series, Working Paper 02-10.

Carroll, R. 2004. *Risk management handbook for health care organizations*, 4th ed. San Francisco: American Society for Healthcare Risk Management, American Hospital Association Press.

Caudron, S. 2004. Jac Fitz-enz, metrics maverick. *Workforce Management* (April): 49–52.

Clark, W. 1999. The Global Environmental Assessment Project: Learning from efforts to link science and policy in an interdependent world. *Acclimations*, Newsletter of the U.S. National Assessment of the Potential Consequences of Climate Variability and Change.

Condron, D. 2000. Recruitment and retention of quality teachers. Testimony before Subcommittee on Postsecondary Education, Training and Life-Long Learning.

Delisio, E.R. 2003. Pay for performance: What are the issues? *Education World* (January 27).

deLoach, J.W., Jr. 2000. *Enterprise-wide risk management: Strategies for linking risk and opportunity*. London: Financial Times.

Friedel, W.F. The efficient risk frontier theory. 2001. *John Liner Review* 15, no. 3 (Fall): 63.

Gladwell, M. 2006. Game theory. *New Yorker* (May 29). Retrieved from www.newyorker.com/critics/content/articles/060529crbo_books1.

Joint Commission on Accreditation of Healthcare Organizations. 2005a. Healthcare at the crossroads: Strategies for improving the medical liability system and preventing patient injury.

Joint Commission on Accredication of Healthcare Organizations. 2005b. Medical liability system hinders improvements in patient safety: Joint Commission expert panel offers solutions to crisis. Press release (February 10).

Lencsis, P.M. 1998. *Workers compensation: A reference guide*. Westport, CT: Quorum Books.

Lewis, M. 2004. *Moneyball: The art of winning an unfair game.* New York: W.W. Norton.

Moorhead, G., and R. Griffin. 1995. *Organizational behavior: Managing people and organizations,* 4th ed. Princeton, NJ: Houghton Mifflin.

Olin, M. 2003. Workers compensation claims—Controlling the costs. *Risk Alert* 2, issue 7 (December).

OMB (Office of Management and Budget). 2001. Memorandum for the heads of executive departments and agencies. Washington, DC: U.S. Government Printing Office.

OPM (Office of Personnel Management). 1996. Workforce Performance Resources Newsletter.

Recruiting Roundtable. 2004. Quality of Hire quantitative initiative. White paper (May 18).

Rotherham, A. 2000. Don't worry, performance pay is coming. *Chicago Tribune.*

Rothstein, R. 2000. Making a case against performance pay. *New York Times.*

Scherkenbach, W. 1988. *The Deming route to quality and productivity.* Washington, DC: CEEPress Books.

Schultz, Theodore. *Investing in people: The economics of population quality.* Berkeley, Calif.: University of California, 1981, p. 21.

Sobel, D. 2005. *Longitude: The true story of a lone genius who solved the greatest scientific problem of his time.* New York: Walker & Company.

Spencer, L.M., and S.M. Spencer. 2001. *Competence at work.* New York: John Wiley & Sons.

SPSS, Inc. 2000. Performance Metrics Jumpstart for Academic Institutions. www.ssps.com.

Stengel, G. 2001. Ten tips for measuring and improving performance. www.stengelsolutions.com.

Stewart, T. 1996. Taking on the last bureaucracy. *Fortune.*

Sullivan, J. 2002. HR metrics the world class way. Peterborough, NH: Kennedy Information.

Swanson, R.A. 1998. Demonstrating the financial benefit of HRD: Status and update on the theory and practice. *Human Resources Quarterly* 9: 285–295.

Taleb, N.N. 2005. *Fooled by randomness: The hidden role of chance in life and in the markets.* New York: Random House.

Teplitz, C.J., 1991. *The learning curve deskbook: A reference guide to theory, calculations, and applications.* New York: Quorum Books.

Trimble, D. 1996. How to measure success: Uncovering the secrets of effective metrics. BPR OnLine Learning Center Series.

Tufte, E. 1992. *The visual display of quantitative information.* Cheshire, CT: Graphics Press.

U.S. Government. 2001. No Child Left Behind Act.

U.S. Government. 2006. The President's Management Agenda.

Walker, P.L., W.G. Shenkir, and T.L. Barton. 2002. *Enterprise risk management: Pulling it all together.* Altamonte Springs, FL: Institute of Internal Auditors Research Foundation.

Watson Wyatt Worldwide. 2003. Incorporating human capital into an integrated measurement approach (August).

Wert, K.R., and J.J. Bryan. 2001. *Managing worker's compensation: A guide to injury reduction and effective claim management.* Boca Raton, FL: Lewis Publishers.

Zirkel, P.A. 2004. Principal: The healthy principal—It's the law. *National Association of Elementary School Principals* 83, no. 4: 10–12.

About the Contributing Authors

Nicholas C. Burkholder

Relentless in the pursuit of "what can be," Nick Burkholder is actively engaged in the development and application of performance frameworks that enable individuals and organizations to achieve optimum results. Nick Burkholder is the President of OnPerformance and founder and a trustee of Staffing.org.

Experienced in virtually every aspect of workforce selection and management, Nick completed consulting engagements in nine counties and worked for organizations including the Johnson & Johnson Worldwide Family of Companies, CIGNA Corporation, The Vanguard Group of Investment Companies, and the U.S. Army.

Nick's previous books include On Staffing: Advice and Perspectives from HR Leaders (John Wiley & Sons, 2003) and Outsourcing: The Definitive View, Applications and Implications (John Wiley & Sons, 2006).

Scott Golas

Scott Golas is a Managing Consultant for PA Consulting based in Chicago. In this role, he works to develop and implement human capital solutions that support and accelerate companies' business strategies, and aligns the resources required to drive implementation. Scott earned an M.S. in organizational development from Loyola University of Chicago and a B.S. in manufacturing engineering and technology from Purdue University. Before joining Aon, Scott was Managing Director at Talent divine/MarchFirst, a Chicago B2E company, and was the HRM (Human Resources Management) consulting practice leader for PricewaterhouseCooper's West Region.

Jeremy Shapiro

Jeremy Shapiro is a Vice President at Bernard Hodes Group, where he co-manages the Hodes iQ e-recruiting product suite. Jeremy has coached hundreds of companies through challenging recruiting technology implementations over the past decade. He holds an M.S. in Information Systems from NYU's Stern School of Business.

Robert Yerex, Ph.D.

Dr. Yerex has a Ph.D. in Quantitative Analysis and an MBA in Finance, both from Cornell University. He is an expert in the development of financial and econometric models that relate human resources initiatives to financial and operational results measurable in real dollar returns. At Kronos, Dr. Yerex heads the Research & Analytics team, where he consults with Human Resources, Finance, and Operations executives from firms in a range of industries on how they can effectively manage and optimize their employee assets. In addition to his industry experience, Dr. Yerex taught in the School of Business and Economics at North Carolina A&T State University as an Associate Professor in the areas of Management, MIS, and Business Process Reengineering.

Anthony Roig

Tony is the Director of Recruitment and Retention for Drexel University. He has held positions in testing and HR for more than 20 years and is a regular contributor to Staffing.org. He holds a B.A. in psychology, a Master of Science degree in industrial psychology, and an M.B.A. from Long Island University.

Christy Risser-Milne

Christy's thorough and thoughtful editing and counsel contributed immeasurably to *Ultimate Performance*. Christy has a bachelor's degree in Communication from Goshen College and a Master of Divinity from Associated Mennonite Biblical Seminary in Elkhart, Indiana.

Alissa Stanley

A veteran of both Staffing.org and HRMetrics.org, Alissa helped to codify the research for *Ultimate Performance* and coordinate author contributions. She has a B.A. from Indiana University of Pennsylvania.

Index